HOME DESIGN WORKBOOKS
STORAGE

HOME DESIGN WORKBOOKS
STORAGE

DINAH HALL & BARBARA WEISS

A DK PUBLISHING BOOK

Project Editor POLLY BOYD
Project Art Editor LIZ BROWN
Picture Research ALLY IRESON, JULIA PASHLEY
Location Photography PETER ANDERSON
Studio Photography MATTHEW WARD
Stylists TIFFANY DAVIES, KAY MCGLONE
Production Controller ALISON JONES
Senior Managing Editor MARY-CLARE JERRAM
Managing Art Editor AMANDA LUNN
US Editor LAAREN BROWN

First American Edition, 1997
2 4 6 8 10 9 7 5 3 1

Published in the United States by DK Publishing, Inc.
95 Madison Avenue, New York, New York 10016
Visit us on the World Wide Web at http://www.dk.com

Copyright © 1997 Dorling Kindersley Limited, London
Text copyright © 1997 Dinah Hall

Library of Congress Cataloging-in-Publication Data
Hall, Dinah.
    Storage / by Dinah Hall and Barbara Weiss. -- 1st American ed.
        p.   cm. -- (Home design workbooks)
    ISBN 0-7894-1450-3
    1. Storage in the home.   I. Weiss, Barbara.   II. Title.   III. Series
TX309.H35 1996
648'.8--dc20
                                                                    96-34441
                                                                        CIP

Text film output in Great Britain by R & B Creative Services
Reproduced in Singapore by Pica
Printed in Great Britain by Butler and Tanner

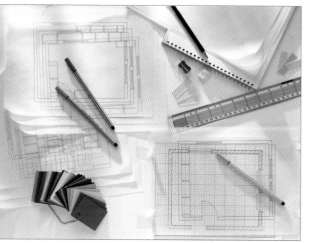

CONTENTS

INTRODUCTION

△ ANTIQUE ARMOIRE
Storage need not be
utilitarian. A decorative
piece of furniture, such
as this Dutch walnut
armoire, may provide
a focal point in the
room as well as serving
a practical function.

SHAKER ROOM ▷
Known for their simple
designs, the Shakers created
a place for everything in
built-in cupboards and
finely crafted stacking boxes.
Portable steps gave access to
high drawers and cabinets.

STORAGE HAS OFTEN been seen as the poor
relation of interior design – a dull but
essential practicality, with little scope for
creativity. But attitudes are changing rapidly –
entire shops dedicated to storage have opened
up, and people are beginning to realize that
organizing their homes to work to maximum
efficiency is an art in itself. Far from tying you
down in domestic detail, well-planned storage
actually allows you to concentrate your energies
in other areas and spend your time in a more
productive way. For those with busy lives, the
old dictum "a place for everything, and
everything in its place" no longer has echoes of
a nagging housekeeper, but offers the welcome
possibility of a stylish refuge from chaos.

Storage is a personal as well as logistical issue, and its implications on your life can be surprisingly far-reaching. Being able to locate articles when you need them, for example, saves time and temper. A living area may be a more or less enjoyable place, depending on how you have arranged storage, while an efficient use of office space is likely to have a positive effect on your working habits. Organizing children's rooms so that they have free access to toys and art materials will improve the quality of their play and thus aid their creative development.

CULTURAL ATTITUDES

Greater awareness of storage needs over the past few years is, of course, related to the fact that we live in an increasingly consumer-driven age. We have vast amounts of goods to store, whereas several hundred years ago the only storage a simple household needed would have been a carved or painted chest in which to keep linens and a few modest belongings. As societies become more affluent, storage becomes not just utilitarian but elaborate – to show off wealth through possessions.

During the second half of the twentieth century, the dynamics of the house changed; the utilitarian rooms that were once taken for granted and associated with drudgery – pantries, laundry rooms, and larders – are now considered a luxury. The modern yearning for living space – the relentless pace at which we have knocked down walls – has been at the expense of those functional rooms, which once acted as a vital support for the smooth running of the house.

Today, these rooms – as well as other dedicated storage areas, such as cellars and lofts – are still invaluable: they take the burden of storage, allowing the other rooms in the house to remain elegant and uncluttered.

The Shakers introduced what might be termed the first real storage "system" in America in the late eighteenth and early nineteenth centuries. Although the Shaker style has since become a fashionable and expensive aesthetic, it was born out of pure practicality. Peg rails attached to the walls provided a convenient place to hang chairs when sweeping the floor, and built-in, as opposed to freestanding, furniture

△ MAJORCAN PANTRY
The ultimate in built-in storage is found in vernacular architecture, where shelves and recesses are molded out of thick plaster or mud walls. Here, the lower niches were originally bread ovens.

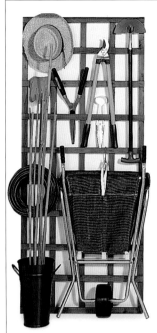

△ IMPROVISED SOLUTION
Costly commercial storage
can sometimes be bypassed
in favor of cheaper, more
creative systems, such as this
wooden trellis. Tools are
hung by butchers' hooks or
tucked behind the trellis.

made rooms easier to clean as well as leaving
the space uncluttered for prayer meetings.

Although the Shakers' views on storage came
through their work ethic, they had much in
common with the traditional Japanese interiors,
which arrived at the same kind of simplicity
from a cultural and hygienic starting point.
Hoarding possessions was alien to the Japanese
mentality – they would have only one individual
object in the traditional display recess called the
"tokonoma," since they considered that only in
its solitary state could the object be fully
appreciated and inspire contemplation.
Belongings associated with everyday living,
such as futons, were stored in another
recess, concealed behind sliding doors.

WHAT DO YOU WANT FROM YOUR STORAGE?

Establish what function you need from your storage: this narrows your options and gives
you a basis for decision. Display demands some kind of shelving, for example, whereas
organization often requires fixtures tailored to your needs.

❶ ORGANIZATION

❷ CONCEALMENT

❸ DISPLAY

❹ PROTECTION

❺ SAFEKEEPING

❻ A FOCAL POINT

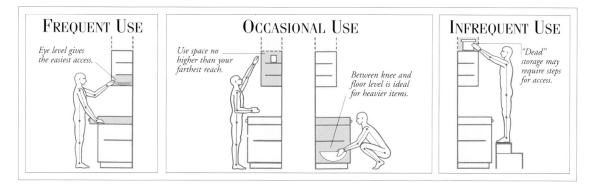

FREQUENT USE

Eye level gives the easiest access.

OCCASIONAL USE

Use space no higher than your farthest reach.

Between knee and floor level is ideal for heavier items.

INFREQUENT USE

"Dead" storage may require steps for access.

◁ **MAXIMUM EFFICIENCY**
For storage to work more efficiently, you need to minimize bending or stretching. Frequently used items should be placed between hip and eye level, while items in occasional use may be stored just above or below this. Less accessible places are ideal for rarely used or seasonal items.

Today, many aspire to this Japanese-style minimalism in their surroundings – but it only works well if you have a ruthless ability to discard extraneous possessions. Storage can certainly help organize an untidy person, but it is unlikely to fundamentally change anyone's character. For this reason, plan your storage, tailoring it as closely as possible to your individual taste, circumstances, personality, and lifestyle, rather than deciding on a "look" dictated by fashion, which may not suit you.

EVALUATING YOUR NEEDS

It is obviously convenient to be able to start from scratch in a new home, designing storage to your own specific requirements. However, in some ways you are at an advantage if you have been living in your home for some time before embarking on any action; you can then see clearly what is not working and why. It might be something as simple as reorganizing your kitchen cabinets so that you are not constantly bending or stretching to awkward heights to reach items in frequent use.

You must first assess the objects you need to store, the reasons for storing them, and how frequently you will need access to them. Luggage that is only used once or twice a year, for example, will obviously have completely different requirements from cleaning or sports equipment that is used on a regular basis. You will want to store some possessions out of sight, while other objects may have an intrinsic display value that you will wish to make the most of.

Assessing your possessions is the ideal opportunity to take stock of how much you

◁ **STRIKING DRESSER**
An original piece of furniture doubling as storage, such as this unique, vividly distressed pink dresser, can set the tone for the whole room. Watch for old pieces in junk shops, or buy unfinished furniture, which you can customize by decorating it yourself.

Full-height cabinets
concealed within the
architecture hide extraneous
clutter, providing the room
with a feeling of space.

ABOUT YOU

An honest appraisal of
your personality and
lifestyle will help you
focus on storage
priorities. Design for
yourself, not the person
you wish you were.
☐ Are you naturally
tidy, or do you need
a storage system that
forces you to organize
your possessions in a
more orderly way?
☐ Do you like to
surround yourself with
objects on display, or do
you prefer a less
cluttered, minimalist
environment?
☐ Are you sharing
storage with someone
who has habits different
from yours?
☐ Do you tend to
collect possessions and
therefore need to plan
for future expansion?
☐ Are your storage
requirements likely to
change? Perhaps you are
planning to start a
family or considering
working from home.
☐ Are you prepared to
clean items on display
regularly, or would your
possessions be better
protected behind doors?

ON DISPLAY ▷
Open shelving and hanging
utensils and herbs create a
cozy, informal kitchen but
need a lot of maintenance
to keep clean and dust-free.

have, and how much you actually need to keep.
Such a suggestion may strike at the very being
of natural hoarders, but there comes a point
when the old has to make way for the new,
and it is clearly a waste of space if something sits
untouched for years. Getting organized often has
an uplifting effect, giving you the energy and
enthusiasm to reevaluate the way you live.

Physically measuring your possessions is often
necessary. Running a tape measure along a row
of hanging clothes to assess the length, or
spreading out all your kitchen equipment on the
floor to get an approximate idea of the number
of square feet it consumes, may seem a tiresome

▽ BUILT-IN BOOKSHELVES
The space above doorways can
often be put to good use:
running shelves all around gives
continuity of plane and an
integrated look to the room.

and time-consuming task, but if you rely on
guesswork you will be surprised at how far off
you are. As a general rule, you can never have
enough storage – empty spaces get filled,
possessions multiply and colonize new areas, so
always leave room for expansion.

DESIGNING WITH STORAGE

Whether you choose built-in or freestanding
storage is very much a matter of personal choice
and budget, but both methods have advantages
and disadvantages (see pp72–73). If space is
limited, you may find that freestanding

cupboards and bookcases restrict circulation; if
you are planning to move, they might be a more
sensible investment, because you can take them
with you. However, your storage must enhance,
not detract from the room, respecting its
architectural and spatial characteristics. Ideally,
built-in storage should look like part of the room
and not as if it has been added on: this may
mean increasing the depth of walls to provide
recessed shelving, and bringing the moldings and
baseboard in front of storage units.

CREATIVE SOLUTIONS

Take a tour of your house, and look for pockets
of space that are not being used – under stairs
and above and around doors, for example. You
might be able to fit a hollow seat under a
window, or extra storage in a platform floor.
Consider also the possibility of constructing a
false ceiling to create a "dead" storage area above.
Be aware of instinctive reactions to space,
however – either side of the chimney may seem
like an obvious place to build shelves, but it
could detract from the beauty of the room by
altering the proportions of the mantelpiece.

Specially-designed storage should contribute
to the mood you wish to create in a room – a
minimalist sanctuary with everything hidden
from view, or a cozy, cluttered atmosphere with
all your possessions on display. Whatever look
you hope to achieve, this book will help and, we
hope, inspire you to rethink the way your
possessions are currently organized, identify your
needs, and plan storage to match your individual
personality, lifestyle, and expectations.

PLAN OF ACTION

Before making any
important decisions
concerning your storage
facilities, read through
the following checklist
to make sure that you
have considered all the
practical requirements.
☐ Establish exactly what
you need to store. Do
you really have to keep
it all, or can you dispose
of anything?
☐ Compile a list with
dimensions of what you
want to store.
☐ Appraise the house
for potential storage
areas that may have
been overlooked.
☐ Establish whether you
will need to access items
frequently or not.
☐ Decide which objects
you wish to display and
which are better hidden.
☐ Consider the design
options (see pp72–79),
and think about which
type of storage will suit
you best.
☐ Evaluate the costs of
each different option.
☐ If you cannot afford
new storage, organize
your belongings more
efficiently in your
current storage space.

ASSESS YOUR NEEDS

THE FOLLOWING questions will prompt you to consider your needs
room by room, so that as you work through this book you will be
able to identify the storage solutions that suit you best.

KITCHEN

The frequency of your shopping trips,
the way you cook, and your preferred
style of kitchen will influence the
organization of your storage.

☐ Do you shop frequently? Or do you
restrict shopping trips to bulk-buying
expeditions once a week or every two
weeks, so you need more storage space?
☐ If you buy large quantities of frozen
foods, does your freezer have the capacity
to store it all? If you prefer fresh foods, do
you have a large refrigerator?
☐ Are your food cabinets and refrigerator
within a few steps of the preparation area?
☐ Are items of food well organized, so that
they are as easy to find as possible?
☐ Do you have space within the kitchen or
another room to create a pantry?
☐ Have you accumulated a lot of cooking
equipment? Could less frequently used
items be stored on high shelves?
☐ Can you reach cooking utensils without
moving from the stove?
☐ Do you make unnecessary trips to fill
pans with water? Could some pans be
stored more conveniently close to the sink?
☐ Do you eat in the kitchen, or do you
have a dedicated dining area where you
could keep some of your dishes?
☐ If you like the informal look of a dresser
and open shelves, do you have time to
clean the objects on display regularly?
☐ Have you allowed space to store non-
food associated equipment, such as cook-
books and items for recycling?

LIVING AREAS

Storage in living areas depends on how
you spend your leisure time, the
amount of items you wish to display,
and whether it is a dual-function room.

☐ Do you have to consider storage for
relaxation and leisure pursuits, or does your
living room double as a dining room?
☐ If you dine in the living area, are the
dish cabinets conveniently located for the
kitchen, and are there enough surfaces on
which to put down dishes?
☐ Are you a collector of books? If so, do
you own mainly reference books, which
require considerably deeper shelves, or
chiefly paperbacks?
☐ Do you own old or valuable books or
ornaments, which would benefit from the
protection of glass-fronted cabinets?
☐ Do you mind your television out in the
open, or would you prefer to conceal it?
☐ Can you adapt existing pieces of
furniture for storage of your sound system
and television, or would built-in cabinets,
which could also house your book
collection, be a better solution?
☐ Do you have a collection that requires
display shelving, and have you allowed for
its expansion? Will you be using lighting to
highlight your display?
☐ Do you need to incorporate office space
into the living area, without detriment to
the primary function of relaxing?

BATHROOM

A room used only for adult washing
and grooming will have very different
storage needs from one catering to the
diverse requirements of a family.

☐ If your bathroom is likely to be used by
visitors, have you considered how much of
the contents you prefer to conceal?
☐ Do you share the bathroom with
children and need to include high or even
lockable storage for medicines and razors?
☐ Is your towel bar placed within reach of
the tub or shower, and is it large enough
to hold the number of towels that you
need to store at any one time?
☐ Do you have the space for a large, dry
closet for storage of spare towels, or will
they have to be stored elsewhere?
☐ Have you made provisions for clothes,
such as hooks for bathrobes, and a laundry
hamper and chair for when you undress?
☐ Are your soaps, sponges, and shampoos
within easy reach of the tub or shower,
and could they be better organized?
☐ Do you have enough shelves, cabinets,
and wall-mounted bathroom accessories
to keep the sink surface from becoming
too cluttered?
☐ Is your storage provision for grooming
activities, such as makeup and shaving,
close to good lighting and a mirror?

BEDROOM

Storage in the bedroom depends on where and how you prefer to store your clothes and the size of room. You will also need to plan for bedside items.

☐ Do you have the space to accommodate a walk-in closet or dressing room?
☐ Is there enough clearance around your bed for a closet with side-hinged doors, or do you need sliding ones?
☐ What ratio of hanging space to shelving or drawers do your clothes currently require, and have you allowed for future expansion of your collection?
☐ Have you a shelf or nightstand for depositing items needed at night or first thing in the morning?
☐ If you have valuables that you wish to store in the bedroom, is it worth investing in a safe for security reasons?
☐ Have you made provision for storage of bulky items, such as extra bedding?
☐ Is there space under the bed that might be used for out-of-season storage?
☐ Do you have a spare bedroom that could hold spillover from other rooms?

CHILD'S ROOM

The ages of your children, and whether they share or have rooms of their own, will determine how you organize their toys, clothes, and other belongings.

☐ Do your children have a separate playroom, or will storage of toys and arrangement of playing space be key factors in their bedrooms?
☐ If the room is to be shared by two or more children, have you considered their separate, age-related needs? Will you have to keep certain toys out of reach of a younger child for safety reasons?
☐ Is shelving organized so that a child can play independently, with easy access to appropriate toys but with restricted access to precious or fragile items?
☐ Do you have a variety of different-sized containers to cope with the range in scale of children's toys?
☐ Is there space under the bed to stow storage crates for toys?
☐ Have you allowed for a quiet study area for an older child?
☐ Are clothes stored at the correct height, so that children can be encouraged to put away their own clothes?

HOME OFFICE

How you store your office equipment, stationery, and papers depends on the nature of your work, and whether you have the luxury of a separate room.

☐ Do you have a room that is dedicated entirely to office use, or does your work space form part of another room?
☐ Is storage planned ergonomically, in order to limit the number of times you need to leave your desk?
☐ If the room is dual-purpose, will you be able to put your work away easily when you require the room for domestic use?

☐ Do you have adequate storage space for extra stationery supplies?
☐ For filing considerations, do you use predominantly legal or letter size?
☐ Are there enough firm surfaces for computers and fax machines?
☐ Do you have sufficient desk space, or would you benefit from wall-mounted swivel platforms to house large pieces of equipment, such as computers?
☐ Do you have technical equipment that will need specialized storage?

OTHER SPACES

Your style of house will dictate whether you have an attic or basement, but you can often find space elsewhere or sacrifice another room for storage.

☐ Are there any "dead" spaces around the house, such as on landings or under stairs, that may offer up storage opportunities?
☐ Are the conditions in the chosen area suitable for the items you are storing?
☐ Are access and lighting good enough to allow for convenient retrieval of items?
☐ Have you protected items in long-term storage from dust and insects?
☐ Would it be helpful to make an inventory of items in long-term storage?
☐ If you have a utility room, can it be used for things other than laundry, such as pet care and outdoor clothing?

HOW THIS BOOK WORKS

THIS BOOK PROVIDES the information you need to make the most of your living space when planning storage for a whole room or adapting existing areas. A series of questions helps you assess your requirements. Then the main part of the book reveals practical solutions for every room in the house. Three-dimensional drawings show storage in context and explain how to achieve a successful design. Finally, instructions on drawing up a plan enable you to translate ideas into reality.

2. CONSIDER THE OPTIONS ▽

The main part of the book (*Storage Solutions, pp16–69*) is organized room by room. Each room chapter is then divided into items to be stored – cooking equipment, clothes, or toiletries, for example. Color photographs show a range of design options, fittings, and accessories available, and simple illustrations indicate ideal heights or depths for storage, when relevant. A "Remember" box draws your attention to the key points to consider.

1. IDENTIFY YOUR NEEDS ▽

A series of preliminary questions encourages you to think about your individual storage needs (*see pp12–13*). By examining aspects of your lifestyle that you take for granted, such as your shopping habits, how tidy you are, and the way in which your possessions are currently organized, you will be able to identify the methods of storage that suit you best.

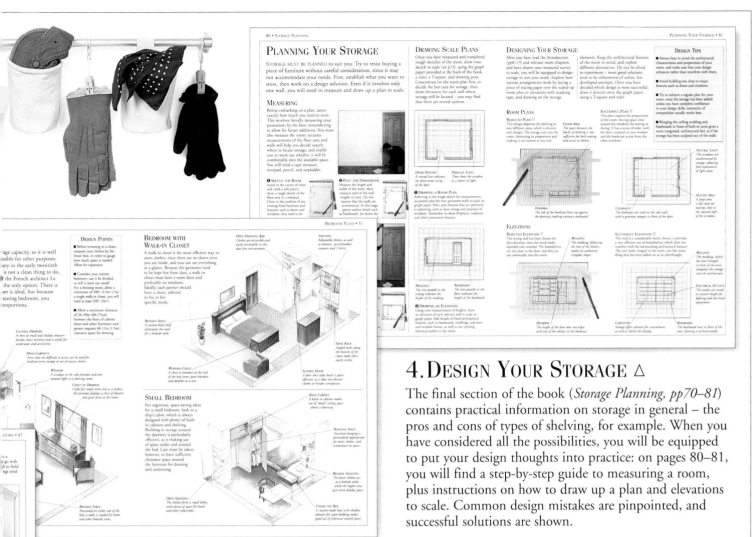

4. DESIGN YOUR STORAGE △

The final section of the book (*Storage Planning, pp70–81*) contains practical information on storage in general – the pros and cons of types of shelving, for example. When you have considered all the possibilities, you will be equipped to put your design thoughts into practice: on pages 80–81, you will find a step-by-step guide to measuring a room, plus instructions on how to draw up a plan and elevations to scale. Common design mistakes are pinpointed, and successful solutions are shown.

3. PLAN IN YOUR STORAGE △

Within each room chapter, three-dimensional drawings offer advice and inspiration on how to design successful storage, taking into account the room's size or shape, or the lifestyle and demands of the occupants. Detailed annotation picks out the main storage elements and their position within the room, and a list of design points highlights the key issues that you need to consider when planning storage for a particular room.

HOW TO USE THE GRAPH PAPER

■ To help you establish the best place to site your storage within the room, draw up your room to scale (*see pp80–81*), using the graph paper provided (*pp89–96*). You may photocopy it if you need more.

■ For a room with small dimensions, use the graph paper with an imperial scale of 1:24, where one large square represents 1ft and a small square 3in. Alternatively, use the metric scale of 1:20, where one large square represents 1m and one small square represents 10cm.

■ For a room with greater dimensions, use the imperial graph paper with the scale of 1:48, where one large square represents 4ft and a small square 6in. Alternatively, use the metric graph paper with the smaller scale of 1:50. Again, the large squares represent 1m and the small squares 10cm.

■ With the room plotted on graph paper, experiment with various storage designs on a tracing paper overlay.

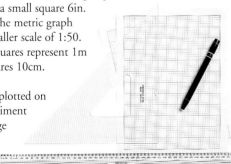

KITCHEN

WE EXPECT MORE from the kitchen than from any other room in the house. It must, of course, be efficient and clean, but the kitchen is no longer a place of solitary confinement for the cook. Perhaps it is where you eat and the children play; bill-paying and homework may have to be accommodated, too. It must also hold a vast range of items requiring different conditions – food and drink, pots and pans, and cook-books. To fulfill such complex and varied demands, you should plan your storage with precision, to be sure that every item is kept where it is most often needed.

TABLEWARE

ORGANIZE YOUR TABLEWARE according to how often you use it – store dishes and cutlery in everyday use at convenient heights near the dishwasher to speed loading and unloading, while specialty items that are used only occasionally may be tucked farther away.

DISHES

Some dishes are purely practical, while other pieces have a decorative value. Ideally, kitchen storage should incorporate open shelves for display, glass-fronted cabinets for protected display, and solid cabinets for concealment. Hooks attached to the edges of shelves are useful for cups and mugs.

△ TRADITIONAL HUTCH
A hutch provides a strikingly decorative and practical "still life." Hutches are best for dishes that are in frequent use, as items on display must be kept clean.

◁ BUILT-IN CABINETS
A combination of different sizes allows you to have a kitchen tailor-made to your needs. Opt for shallow units over the work surface – they allow more headroom and the contents are easier to reach.

REMEMBER

■ Open shelves are attractive for displaying dishes and make frequently used items accessible, but pieces are exposed to dust and grease. Position open shelves away from steamy areas like the stove or sink.

■ Allocate items to the correct depth of shelf. Avoid deep dish cabinets where smaller items, such as tea cups, invariably become lost behind piles of larger plates.

■ Plate racks offer storage while providing an attractive and practical way of draining dishes.

CUTLERY

The method of storage you use for your cutlery will depend on how and where you use it. For everyday cutlery, a shallow drawer makes the best use of space, and its contents can be seen at a glance. For items that are more valuable or less frequently used, choose specialized drawers or chests.

◁ TIERED DRAWER
This special tiered cutlery rack makes good use of a deep drawer. In a standard cutlery tray, where everything is jostled together, it is difficult to keep cutlery in order: here, separate grooves for each piece prevent damage.

CHROME BASKET
A nonrusting metal basket drains cutlery hygienically.

△ SILVERWARE CHEST
Silver cutlery needs special care. Clean before storing and wrap in acid-free tissue away from direct sunlight and damp. Do not store stainless steel and silver together.

△ CUTLERY BASKET
If you don't have a dishwasher, a drainer basket is useful for air-drying. It is also convenient for carrying cutlery from the dish-washing area to the table or drawer.

PERISHABLE FOOD

JUGGLING THE DEMANDS of today's busy lifestyles requires careful planning and food storage: we tend to shop less often than we used to and keep food for longer periods of time, while growers' use of fewer preservatives mean that food may not last as long. Consumer awareness of health issues has provoked an interest in optimizing storage conditions to preserve freshness in the most natural way possible.

FRESH FOOD

Storage conditions for fresh foods can vary greatly according to climate and season. Potatoes, for example, tend to sprout in spring even when kept under ideal conditions, so it is wise to buy smaller quantities in warmer seasons. Be aware of the life cycles of fresh food.

HANGING RACK
A rack is convenient for utensils and foods that need ventilation, such as garlic.

VEGETABLE BASKETS ▷
The renaissance of the basket for storing food over the last few years may be an aesthetic reaction against technology, but there are practical advantages, too. Baskets allow air to circulate, which, combined with darkness, is perfect for root vegetables like potatoes or carrots.

WICKER BASKETS
Kept in a dark, cool place, baskets are useful for root vegetables, onions, or bread.

CURTAIN
Hide-all gingham curtain heightens rustic charm.

REMEMBER

■ If you are short of floor space, try a hanging basket for fruit and vegetables.

■ Use food for decorative purposes: a bowl of fruit is both attractive and accessible.

■ Analyze your shopping and cooking habits before deciding which refrigerator to buy. If you shop often and eat more fresh than frozen food, you will want a proportionally bigger refrigerator than freezer.

■ For food safety, refrigerator temperatures should be 34–41°F (1–5°C); always keep raw and cooked foods separate.

ADJUSTABLE SHELVES
Wire baskets can be
moved easily for storage
and for washing.

△ PULL-OUT VEGETABLE BIN

If you like the practical qualities of traditional wicker baskets but feel that they would look out of place in a modern streamlined kitchen, consider installing a concealed system that fits neatly beneath the work surface.

△ BREAD-BOX DRAWER

Keeping bread in its own drawer frees up valuable space on the work surface. These terra-cotta bins keep bread fresh and allow removal of crumbs. You could adapt a deep drawer in a similar manner.

CHILLED AND FROZEN FOOD

The era of the iceman is long gone, and even the irksome yet strangely rewarding task of defrosting the freezer may soon become a part of history. Most homes now offer the convenience of ample refrigeration and freezer storage. With advances in technology, there is an ever-increasing variety of appliances on the market to suit a diverse range of lifestyles and cooking habits.

◁ **REFRIGERATED DRAWERS**
These are an ingenious, if costly, innovation since fresh food can be stored in them at various strategic points around the kitchen. Refrigerator drawers vary in temperature and humidity – here, the bottom drawer has a relative humidity of up to 90 percent, which is ideal for keeping fruit and vegetables fresh and crisp. Freezer drawers are also available.

DAIRY PRODUCTS
Keep cheese and butter in
an airtight box, away from
other foods, to prevent strong
flavors from affecting them.

REFRIGERATOR ▷
Food must be stored at the right temperature to avoid contamination. A combination refrigerator-freezer, in which the proportion of refrigerator to freezer can vary according to your eating patterns, is the most popular choice for family kitchens.

UNCOOKED MEAT
Keep raw meat wrapped
and on the lowest shelf to
avoid contaminating
food below.

VEGETABLES
Store green vegetables
loose in a vegetable box,
and salad vegetables in
an airtight container.

FROZEN FOOD
Freeze foods in regular
packages to make best use
of space, and label clearly.

NONPERISHABLE FOOD

CHANGES IN WORKING PATTERNS and consumer habits have dramatically altered the way we plan our kitchens. The tendency to do one big weekly supermarket run means that we need more storage space than in previous generations, when people shopped almost daily. An interest in unusual cuisines also demands more space for spices and condiments.

FOOD

Divide groceries into categories – jars, cans, baking ingredients, and dry goods – and plan space for them according to use. Foods that go straight into a saucepan can be kept near the stove, for example. Store frequently used items in the most accessible places, and sort by size and shape for easy retrieval.

PANTRY SHELVING ▷
If you have generous storage space, it makes sense to buy staples in bulk so that you can improvise meals without panic trips to the store. But check your shelves periodically – sell-by dates assume optimum conditions, and many dry goods have a surprisingly short shelf life.

REMEMBER

■ Your storage arrangements should reflect your shopping habits. The less frequently you shop, the more storage space you will need.

■ Glass jars containing pasta or spices make an appealing display, but need regular maintenance – they do not look attractive when they are less than half full.

■ Ideally, food cabinets should be sited away from stove or refrigerator exhausts, and they must be kept cool, dry, and clean. There are a variety of tiered shelf units that fit into cabinets to raise cans and small items, making them accessible.

■ Check contents every few months for products that are past their sell-by date, and rotate stock in cabinets regularly so that food does not become forgotten.

■ Dried herbs and spices and dry foods such as rice, pasta, flour, and dried fruit should be stored in airtight containers, preferably in cabinets, as their flavors are affected by light, heat, and moisture.

CLOSED DOORS
These elegant paneled doors banish the workaday atmosphere of a kitchen.

OPEN DOORS
The doors open and slide back along the sides of the cabinet when in use.

◁ △ **CONCEALED PANTRY**
A pantry behind closed doors solves the problem of unsightly objects that need to be stored in a kitchen, but are hardly necessary when the room is used for entertaining. It is an arrangement that works well in studios or other spaces where you do not want the mechanics of the kitchen to intrude in the room.

△ **DISPLAY SHELVING**
Consistency in the type of
storage jars used, like these
artists' paint jars, gives a
pleasing uniformity to open
shelves. Display only small
quantities of frequently used
spices, since they deteriorate
on exposure to light.

HIGH SHELF
Extra space at the top of the
cabinet is ideal for long-term
storage of bottles.

ADJUSTABLE BASKETS
Easily movable, these baskets
can accommodate a variety
of different-sized groceries.

INTERNAL FRAMEWORK
The pantry cabinet pulls out
on sturdy tracks so that the
food can be seen at a glance.

PULL-OUT PANTRY ▷
A tall, narrow cabinet that
pulls out is an excellent use
of space, as the contents are
accessible from both sides
of the unit – for this reason,
they should never be built
into a corner. Pull-out pantries
are available in various widths
and heights. Some models fit
beneath the countertop.

DRINK

Most drinks are best stored in cool conditions,
away from the warmth of heating and lighting. For
short-term storage, keep bottles no higher than waist
height to prevent breakage, but not so low that retrieval
is difficult – between 28in (70cm) and 35in (90cm) is
ideal. Do not stack bottles too tightly or too deeply –
a cabinet designed for the purpose is ideal.

WINE CELLAR ▷
Catering equipment like
this wine cellar, which
allows for precise
temperature control,
is increasingly finding
its way into domestic
situations. Its glass front
can add interest to a
monotonous landscape
of solid kitchen cabinets.

SHELVES
Closely spaced, ridged
shelves keep bottles
firmly in position.

WINE RACK
Store wine horizontally in racks in a
cool, dark place away from foot traffic.

MOBILE CART
Bottles are easier to find in a
pull-out box on casters than
in a low, deep cabinet.

△ **BOTTLE STORAGE**
Bottles are cumbersome objects to store and transport, so consider
some form of movable storage. Wine is better left undisturbed: ideally,
most wines should be stored in a cellar at 50–59°F (10–15°C), but
the kitchen is adequate for short-term storage of inexpensive wines.

COOKING EQUIPMENT

EVEN THE MOST reluctant cook tends to accumulate a vast collection of equipment, ranging in size from large appliances such as food processors to tiny utensils like carrot peelers. Storage for each piece should reflect where and how often it is used – close to the preparation area with an electrical outlet nearby, or by the sink or stove.

POTS AND PANS

The variety of shapes, sizes, and frequency of use suggest pans should be stored in differing locations. Saucepans in daily use should be within easy reach of the stove – perhaps hanging from a rack. Others can be kept in cabinets or on pan racks.

COUNTERPOINT ▷
An old cupboard with doors and drawers may be just as efficient a means of storage as a sleek row of modern cabinets – and considerably cheaper. Combined with a shelf, a rack, and wall-mounted accessories, it offers a surprisingly large amount of storage as well as an adequate work surface for a small kitchen.

△ UNDER-STOVE RACKS
Sturdy metal slatted shelves beneath the stove save opening doors to reach pans while cooking, and provide a convenient drying place for washed pans and cookie sheets. However, they are exposed to dust and grease, so are best for items that are frequently used. For greater, longer-term protection, store pans in deep drawers or in pull-outs.

TERRA-COTTA JAR
Keep wooden spoons and other utensils in a jar close to the stove and preparation area.

WORK SURFACE
Try to keep counters clear of items that are not in daily use.

LOW SHELF
Heavy dishes are easier to lift from a low position.

PAN LID RACK
Curtain wire strung inside a cabinet door is a simple device for storing lids.

HIGH SHELF
For bulky items that are not too heavy, a high shelf is ideal. Many pans have a sculptural display value.

HANGING RACK
Lightweight pans, utensils, and even certain vegetables in daily use are easily accessible from a hanging rack.

KITCHEN CABINETS

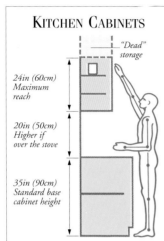

"Dead" storage

24in (60cm) Maximum reach

20in (50cm) Higher if over the stove

35in (90cm) Standard base cabinet height

Store frequently used items such as food and utensils within easy reach. Keep bulk groceries and rarely used equipment in the "dead" area above 6ft 6in (2m).

REMEMBER

■ Try to relate the positioning of storage facilities to the use of equipment – colanders and strainers might be kept by the sink; pans should be stored close to the stove; and baking items are best near the preparation area.

■ Allow sufficient electrical outlets and counter space for frequently used appliances. Permanent counter space should be allocated only to kitchen equipment that is used on a daily basis.

■ Avoid stacking pots and pans: they may scratch, and suction can make it difficult to separate them.

■ Do not store sharp knives loose in drawers – keep them away from children in knife blocks or on magnetic strips.

UTENSILS AND APPLIANCES

With the wide selection of gadgets on the market, it is sensible to weigh their convenience value against the amount of space they consume. You could give permanent residence at the back of the counter to one or two appliances in daily use, as most activity is contained within the front two-thirds of the counter.

APPLIANCE GARAGE ▷
A tambour shutter pulls down for a quick visual clean-up. Shelves – some divided into small compartments – provide storage for a selection of items, and a counter with electrical outlets allows appliances to remain plugged in, so that they are ready for use.

ATTACHMENTS
Food processor attachments are stored beneath the shelf at the base of the cabinet.

UTENSIL RACK ▷
Hanging small gadgets and utensils on a rack makes them easily visible, and eliminates rummaging in an overcrowded drawer. Wooden slats or a metal grid hung with butchers' hooks make use of wall storage space that is otherwise wasted.

◁ FOOD PROCESSOR UNIT
For many, food processors are an essential piece of kitchen apparatus, but they are extremely cumbersome and awkward to store. If you do not want your equipment as a permanent fixture on the counter, but use it frequently enough that it needs to be easily accessible, this innovative fitting is the solution.

PLATFORM SHELF
The shelf that houses the food processor lifts up and out of the cabinet to provide extra work space.

KITCHEN PLANS

IN THE PAST, THE KITCHEN used to be located as far as possible from the main part of the house and was out of bounds for most family members. Today, however, the kitchen is often strategically and emotionally at the heart of the home. Its design must reflect your personal lifestyle: take into account the size of your family, your shopping, cooking, and eating habits, and the activities you intend to undertake in the room. A new kitchen is one of the most expensive alterations you can make to your home, so time given to careful planning is a worthwhile investment.

CASUAL KITCHEN

For some, the nostalgic comfort of the "farmhouse kitchen," where you can eat and relax as well as cook, outweighs the appeal of efficient, modern units. A collection of freestanding furniture, such as a dresser and cupboard, combined with hanging racks for pots and pans, will provide adequate storage as long as you do not own a huge amount of equipment and appliances. Ideally, you should have the backup that a traditional farmhouse kitchen would have enjoyed – a cool pantry, to keep fresh foods below room temperature.

DESIGN POINTS

■ When planning your kitchen, make sure that the cooking, washing, and food preparation areas are no more than a few steps apart, to avoid wasted trips across the room.

■ Consider the maximum number of people who will be working in the kitchen at one time, and allow for adequate circulation in front of cabinets.

■ Do not forget kitchen trash. A concealed garbage can by the sink is fine for small families; if you generate a large amount of trash, consider a compactor.

PLATE RACK
A wooden rack doubles as storage and drip-dry facility for dishes.

HANGING RACK
A strong rack for pans makes use of otherwise wasted ceiling space.

HANGING BAR
Located above the stove, a bar keeps utensils and small pans close at hand.

CONVERTED ARMOIRE
Equipped with shelves, an old armoire makes a good store for kitchen equipment.

DRESSER
A traditional dresser provides concealed storage as well as display potential.

BUTCHER'S BLOCK
A traditional butcher's block offers a firm surface for chopping; many have a special slot for knife storage.

GALLEY KITCHEN

The galley layout is found in many modern homes where space is limited. Its compactness works in its favor from an ergonomic point of view: everything is close at hand, so little time and energy are wasted in locating what you require. You need to make good use of wall space in a small kitchen, so upper cabinets are usually necessary. The central aisle should be no narrower than 35in (90cm).

REFRIGERATOR-FREEZER
A tall, narrow refrigerator-freezer maximizes storage space for fresh food.

FOOD CABINET
Provide sufficient cabinet space for groceries in a small kitchen.

OPEN SHELF
A display shelf prevents a modern galley kitchen from looking too clinical.

UTENSIL JAR
A decorative earthenware jar keeps wooden spoons within easy reach of the stove.

DISH CABINETS
Store dishes and glassware close to the dishwasher for convenience when unloading.

ABOVE-OVEN CABINET
The cabinet above the oven is hinged at the top, allowing easy access to baking sheets and pans.

LARGE KITCHEN

In a household where the kitchen is the hub of the home, a large room is ideal: it enables people to congregate and allows numerous activities to take place without disturbing the cook. However, a large kitchen must be meticulously planned in order to prevent unnecessary trips back and forth across the room. Island units provide separate work zones as well as storage and make use of otherwise "dead" space in the center of the room.

OPEN SHELVES
A small alcove for mugs and pitchers near the coffeemaker or teapot provides a dedicated coffee or tea corner.

REFRIGERATOR
The modern refrigerator has a large capacity for food.

CLEARING AWAY AREA
A large unit contains a trash compactor, garbage disposal, and dishwasher.

PANTRY CABINET
A mini pantry for cans and staples, this cabinet is equipped with shelves and wire baskets.

SINK UNIT
A double sink is located close to the stovetop for maximum convenience.

REFRIGERATED DRAWERS
Chilled drawers store fruit and vegetables within easy reach of the preparation area, avoiding the need to use the main refrigerator.

LIVING AREAS

ROOMS NO LONGER have the rigidly defined functions they once did. A living area may encompass relaxation, dining, entertaining, television viewing, and a multitude of other recreational activities – it may be formal or informal, family-oriented, or a strictly adult space. Inevitably, multipurpose rooms create more complex demands on storage, but with thoughtful use of flexible, adaptable units and accessories to house a diverse range of possessions, you won't need to compromise the look of the room.

EATING AND DRINKING

WHILE MANY PEOPLE enjoy the informality of eating in the kitchen, there are still advantages to having a separate dining room, away from cooking smells and dirty dishes. A dining room also offers space to store many items not in daily use, such as extra dinner services, table linens, and large platters.

DISHES AND GLASSWARE

While some dishes are worth displaying, more utilitarian, everyday china usually requires cabinet space. Traditionally, the dining room sideboard housed the dishes and glassware, but today there are many more flexible solutions.

SHALLOW SHELVES
Stemmed glasses are stored single file to prevent breakage.

DRAWERS
Wide, shallow drawers are ideal for placemats and bulky table linen.

WALL OF CABINETS ▷
Glass-fronted cabinets break up the visual monotony of a row of solid fronts and protect the contents from dust, but the items inside should be visually engaging.

△ VESTRY FURNITURE
The clever adaptation of cupboards and drawers that once graced a church vestry has resulted in an original but wholly workable update on the traditional sideboard. The shallow drawers originally used for vestments are particularly useful for small items, like napkin rings, that easily become lost in deep drawers.

REMEMBER

■ If dining room storage is used as an overspill for the kitchen, try to be sure that you do not have to travel too far from the kitchen to collect and replace glasses and dishes.

■ A living room should be a relaxing, comfortable place. Choose storage that is able to cope efficiently with all the various demands that are placed on the room, without appearing overly utilitarian.

■ Objects that are displayed in a dining room should be appropriate to the general style of the room: if you have a formal dining room, for example, everyday dishes are best concealed in cabinets or a sideboard, or in the kitchen.

DRINK

Drinks that are kept for serving outside the kitchen in living areas tend to be wine, spirits, and mixers. Together with cocktail equipment and glasses, they require their own space – preferably in a locked cabinet, if there are small children in the house.

△ CONCEALED SHELVES
Those who prefer a minimalist environment may choose to incorporate storage into the architecture to conceal all extraneous clutter, without detracting from the proportions of the room. The designer of the living room above built a false wall to create elegant, shallow cabinets to house bottles and wine glasses.

WINE CABINET ▷
This unusual cabinet was designed for a wine connoisseur without a cellar. It has its own temperature control, so wine can be kept in a centrally heated room. It also contains a humidor for cigars.

COLLECTIONS

ANY COLLECTION – books, seashells, clocks, or fine porcelain – has intrinsic display value that can be enhanced by a well-lit, complementary setting. Housing your collection within a carefully considered framework brings focus to the objects displayed. Avoid half measures – aim for a graphic display of single objects or go for drama with numbers.

DISPLAYING OBJECTS

Even the most commonplace objects can earn aesthetic status by the way in which they are displayed – while wooden spoons in a jar are utilitarian, arranged in formation on a wall they may be viewed as art. Start by analyzing the objects to be displayed: group by size and color, and consider the most favorable angle for viewing.

RECESSED ALCOVES
Building a false wall creates alcoves, a visually effective way of framing objects.

BRACKET SHELVES
Wall-mounted shelves highlight individual pieces or small groupings.

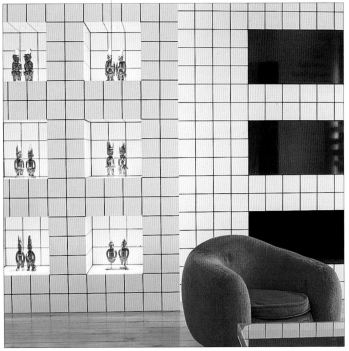

△ **MINIMALIST DISPLAY**
The strong geometric severity of these alcoves, which owe something of their style to retail displays, encourages a changing selection of objects. Alcoves are particularly suitable for single items, or graphic groups, but they require effective accent lighting. In this display, low-voltage downlights draw the eye to the small figures in the niches.

ROOM OF VASES ▷
The collector of this British studio pottery of the late nineteenth and early twentieth century designed his room around the vases, using a combination of antique freestanding cupboards and wall-mounted shelves. The style of furniture should complement the collection: here, the cupboards and vases date from the same period.

BOOKS

Most homes accumulate huge numbers of books, which can be extremely heavy. Be sure that your shelves are attached securely to structurally sound walls, with supports at regular intervals (*see p75*). If you are using freestanding shelves, check that the floor is load-bearing. Never expose books to damp or excessive heat.

▽ **WALL-TO-WALL DISPLAY**
Built-in shelves must fit in with architectural features: here, shallow shelves on either side of the deeper central shelves do not obstruct the window. Keep a set of steps on hand for access to books on the high shelves.

ATLAS SHELF
A closely spaced shelf is designed to accommodate a world atlas.

BUILT-IN CABINETS
Low cabinets store drinks, games, and a sound system.

SHALLOW SHELVES
Shallow shelves are ideal for small books, like paperbacks.

REMEMBER

■ Collections do not remain static: allow for expansion by providing up to 50 percent more space than you estimate is needed initially.

■ If you cannot afford built-in lighting, consider other ways to enhance objects: painting the interiors of niches is effective.

■ Books and objects to be displayed vary greatly in size: adjustable shelves or niches of differing dimensions are more flexible than fixed shelves.

■ Store books upright – it damages them if they are too crowded or too loose. As a rough guide, allow 1in (2.5cm) between the top of the books and the next shelf. If you only have a few outsize books, stack them horizontally.

△ **FREESTANDING BOOKCASES**
The advantage of freestanding bookcases is that, unlike built-in shelves, you can take them with you if and when you move. They may be quite dominant, so they should fit in stylistically with the architecture of the room. Glass fronts are ideal, as they protect books from dust.

ENTERTAINMENT

RELAXATION INCLUDES the active pursuit of hobbies and games as well as passive pleasures offered by television and sound systems. As a result, living rooms often have to contain a disparate combination of old-fashioned adult games and high-tech equipment.

TELEVISION AND MUSIC

In many homes, the television has replaced the fireplace as the focal point of a room, but various storage options can lessen its impact. Modern sound systems are now so compact that they are more easily incorporated into a room than older models.

CD RACK ▷
You can make a strong visual statement by storing CDs in a sculptural rack, rather than concealing them. The design of this quirky alligator makes CDs easily accessible.

◁ **SPECIALLY MADE UNITS**
Mobile television storage is more flexible than a built-in cabinet, as it does not dictate seating. A simple stand on casters, as shown here, is easy to move for viewing or putting away. Freestanding cabinets are useful for an ever-growing collection of videocassettes or CDs.

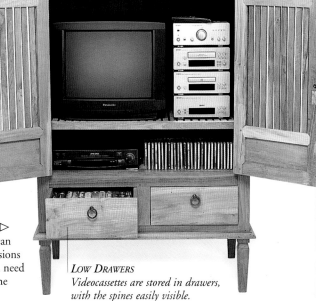

SLATTED DOORS
Electrical equipment needs good ventilation, provided by these slatted wooden doors.

CONVERTED FURNITURE ▷
Old cabinets and armoires can be adapted to conceal televisions and sound systems: you will need to drill holes for wiring at the back and adjust the shelves.

LOW DRAWERS
Videocassettes are stored in drawers, with the spines easily visible.

GAMES AND PASTIMES

Living rooms often have to accommodate a wide-ranging selection of hobby materials – knitting yarn, photograph albums, and games for children and adults. Clutter is not conducive to relaxation, so while these items need to be readily available, they must also be easy to stash away. If you have children, keep a wicker basket in the corner of the room in which to clear away toys.

◁ **GAMES CHEST**
This elegant early nineteenth-century secretary has proved an ideal place to store boxed games, playing cards, and score pads. It has a large flap which, when closed, completely conceals its contents. When open, it reveals a number of drawers – some secret – and alcoves for small items.

DRAWERS
Small drawers are perfect for storing decks of cards, dice, and pads of paper.

RECESS
Small boxed games and leather boxes fit neatly into the central well.

FLAP DOOR
Open flap becomes a playing surface for board games.

△ **SIDE TABLE**
Surfaces for setting down objects are as important as places to put objects away, yet they are often overlooked. A small side table near seating to rest a drink, reading material, or handiwork helps make a room both comfortable and functional.

△ **BOOK BASKET**
A portable basket of children's books is useful in the living room, since it can be moved to where the children are and is easy to tuck away. Baskets are ideal for large, floppy books and small, chunky ones that do not fit easily on shelves; it also means you can quickly identify books by their covers, rather than their spines.

REMEMBER

■ Store your television and sound system near electrical outlets, away from direct heat and sunlight. Because of their magnetic fields, do not put televisions next to unshielded speakers or cast-iron or steel radiators.

■ If you choose to conceal your sound system or television in a cabinet, be sure it is well ventilated. Remote-control systems require a glass-fronted door; they do not work through solid panels.

■ A beautiful piece of furniture with compartments can offer storage for many hobby and craft items, as well as providing a decorative focus.

■ If you do not have a special piece of furniture for your games, hobby items, or videocassettes, try storing them in attractive fabric-covered boxes on open shelving.

LIVING AREAS PLANS

YOUR STORAGE SHOULD contribute to the aesthetics of your living areas, so plan it carefully, and buy the best you can afford. Built-in cabinets can actually improve existing proportions, for example, by making a long, narrow room shorter and by concealing unwanted alcoves or irregularities. Shelving can accentuate the character of a room: if you have a low ceiling, visually strong uprights and shelf dividers may give the illusion of more vertical space. Conversely, you may actually choose to emphasize the horizontality of a room by playing down the vertical supports and using a shelving system with thicker shelves.

LIVING ROOM

The living room should be a place of relaxation and comfort. To achieve this, you have to plan the layout of the room carefully and consider the practicalities of storage – you need somewhere to keep books, a place to house the television, and a surface on which to put down your drink. A combination of built-in shelves and cabinets allows you to display your favorite objects and to conceal others, but they must be designed carefully to complement the architecture of the room.

DESIGN POINTS

■ Avoid placing furniture only around the edges of the room. Storage used as room dividers gives the feeling of more space rather than less.

■ Shelves to accommodate different sizes of books should vary in depth from 9–16in (23–40cm). Stereo equipment and televisions require deep shelves: allow access to sockets and room for wiring and plugs.

■ Provide adequate lighting for your storage, such as directional lights over bookcases and slim-line fluorescents inside cabinets.

RECESSED SHELVES
An alcove is built out to make the shelves look as if they are set into the thickness of the wall.

CABINETS
Elegantly paneled cabinets are built around and above the doorway.

MANTELPIECE
A carefully styled mantelpiece gives focus to the room.

TELEVISION CABINET
A swivel arm angles the set toward viewers and retracts for concealment.

SIDE TABLE
Small tables close to seating are essential for putting down drinks or books.

DINING ROOM

Nowadays, a room dedicated solely to dining is an increasingly rare phenomenon. There are many advantages to having a separate dining room, particularly from the point of view of storage, since it can take the spillover from the kitchen, such as precious china and cutlery and large serving dishes. If the room is at a distance from the kitchen, it makes sense to choose storage with a low, flat surface for resting dishes removed during the meal. A modern, updated version of the old-fashioned sideboard is ideal.

BUILT-IN HOT PLATE
A hot plate keeps food warm and saves unnecessary trips back and forth to the kitchen.

TRAY STORAGE
Keep a selection of trays in the dining room for transporting dirty dishes to the kitchen.

BUILT-IN SIDEBOARD
A combination of cabinets, open shelves, and drawers houses a range of accessories for the table.

TRADITIONAL SIDEBOARD
A dinner service is stored in the sideboard; plates are displayed along the back.

DUAL-FUNCTION ROOM

In modern homes, a separate dining room is rarely an option. If the kitchen is small, the living room will also have to accommodate the dining room table – an arrangement that well-planned storage can ease. Establish the best places for different activities – a convenient spot for eating, a nonfocal point for the television, a desk area – and choose storage that can demarcate the various different areas.

MAGAZINE RACK
Dual-function rooms must remain neat – a rack keeps magazines handy.

MOBILE CART
Useful for table accessories, a cart can be wheeled away when not needed.

CONVERTED CABINET
An old cabinet converted to house stereo equipment and CDs doubles as a television stand.

COFFEE TABLE
Choose a tiered coffee table that offers storage as well as a top surface.

PARTITION SHELVING
Backed up against a sofa, low shelving acts as a room divider and storage place for dishes.

WRITING DESK
Dedicate a corner of the room to personal correspondence and household accounts.

BATHROOM

THE PRIMARY PURPOSE of a bathroom is obvious, but it can be a place of refuge and relaxation if designed with comfort as well as practicality in mind. Ideally, a bathroom should have a combination of open and closed storage to cater to its dual nature: perfumes, lotions, and bath oils on display often contribute to the room's aesthetics, while medicine and cleaning solutions are best concealed in a vanity.

PERSONAL CARE

A BATHROOM conceals, and sometimes reveals, the most intimate truths about personal habits. Bear this in mind if it is a room that is shared with family members, other occupants, or if it is accessible to visitors.

MEDICINE

Most families have to store a vast number of creams and ointments, but the average bathroom cabinet is rarely large enough to contain all this plus bulky objects, such as boxes of tissues or diapers. Built-in cabinets offer a considerable amount of storage; wall-mounted cabinets are a more flexible option.

REMEMBER

■ It is preferable to have several smaller laundry baskets located in different rooms where undressing takes place. One huge Ali-Baba-style basket is not as practical, as it is difficult to transport to and from the washing machine.

■ Keep medicine and other potentially dangerous items in high or lockable cabinets. First-aid kits should be stored where they are easily accessible in case of emergencies.

MEDICINE BOX
Store medications for each member of the family in separate containers – plastic boxes are ideal, as they are easy to clean.

HIDDEN DOORS
Several cabinets without handles offer a large, uninterrupted mirror area.

◁ **WALL-MOUNTED CABINET**
Although built-in cabinets give bathrooms a more integral, streamlined finish, an attractive wall-mounted cabinet, such as the traditional Shaker cupboard shown here, can double as a decorative feature in the room.

△ **MIRRORED CABINETS**
The doors of these bathroom cabinets, some of which are for medicines, open with touch latches to avoid the need for visually intrusive handles. The mirrors add extra light and a sense of space to the room.

LAUNDRY

Households usually generate a phenomenal amount of dirty laundry, which, if no provision is made for it, tends to pile up on bathroom and bedroom floors. To prevent this from happening, place laundry baskets in whichever rooms are used for undressing – and teach your children to use them.

LAUNDRY BAGS ▷
Dividing laundry into loads – hot and cold water, light and dark laundry – saves time in the utility room. The labels on the bags are printed with symbols showing the treatment required.

◁ **LAUNDRY HAMPER**
A built-in hamper is a neat alternative to a laundry basket, particularly in a small room where floor space is limited. The disadvantage is that clothes have to be transferred to another container to be taken to the washing machine.

PULL-OUT DRAWER
Two large pull-down containers separate laundry into dark and white washes.

BATH MAT RACK
Small chrome rack in front of the radiator provides a warm place for drying out a damp bath mat.

WASHING AND DRYING

FEEL LIKE AN ENERGETIC spritz under the shower or a long, relaxing soak in a perfumed bath? Your storage should be organized so that either can be undertaken with minimum mess and maximum efficiency. Whatever the size or style of your bathroom, there should always be adequate, well-placed storage for soaps, shampoos, and towels.

BATHING AND SHOWERING

Try to set aside a specific area for bath or shower accessories. Open shelving is ideal for appealingly packaged products, but you will also need cabinet space for less attractive items that are better concealed.

◁ **RECESSED SHELVING**
If you need more storage in the bathroom and can afford to lose a few inches of floor space, it is possible to build out a wall to create an alcove with shelving. Recessed shelves provide a decorative focus to the room; positioned above the bath, they are also a convenient and practical place to keep accessories that you need for bathing.

DECORATIVE SHELF
Shelves that are out of reach of the bath can be used for display.

ACCESSORY SHELF
Toiletries can quickly clutter up the sides of the bath, so place them on a shelf nearby.

△ **SHOWER CORNER UNIT**
A tiered portable or wall-mounted chrome caddy keeps shower accessories, such as brushes, loofahs, soaps, and shampoos, together and close at hand, and fits snugly in the corner of a shower cubicle. Slatted shelves allow the wet items to drain easily.

△ **BATH RACK**
A rack across the tub is the ideal solution if you do not have built-in storage beside the bath for toiletries. For those who enjoy a leisurely read, this rack has the added advantage of doubling as a book rest.

BATHROOM SHELVING

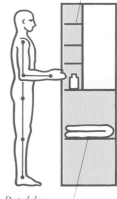

Shallow shelves: depth 3–5in (8–13cm)

Deep shelves: depth 16in (40cm)

Bathroom storage should include shallow shelving for small items, such as toiletries and medicines, and deep cabinets for bulky items, such as towels and toilet paper.

TOWELS

It is awful to sprint across the bathroom, dripping water as you go, to reach for a cold, damp bath towel draped over a clammy towel bar. Storage of towels, both in use and extra supplies, must therefore be a prime consideration in bathroom planning. Taking into account family members and guests, you may have to allow considerable closet space for towels.

◁ **HEATED TOWEL RACK**
In cold or humid climates, where towels take a long time to dry out, a heated rack – electric or connected to the central heating system – is a necessary luxury. This model holds several towels at once.

HIDDEN SHELVING
Unlike hinged doors, this sliding mechanism allows the mirror to be used when open.

CHROME RACK
The rack makes use of space under the sink, while the towels partially hide the plumbing.

HAND TOWEL RACK ▷
In order to avoid ending up with a wet floor, towels should be kept adjacent to washing areas. Here, an integral rack is built into the basin; hooks or wall-mounted towel rods would fulfill the same function.

LINEN BASKET
Wicker baskets are an attractive and portable option for linen and towel storage.

FABRIC FRONT
Curtains guard against dust, conceal clutter, and give a more airy feel than solid doors.

FREESTANDING SHELVING ▷
If your bathroom has good heating and ventilation, you may decide to keep a supply of neatly folded towels on display, although you must be sure that they are used and washed frequently, as they soon become dusty. Freestanding shelf units offer flexibility both in terms of storage and choice of location, but they do take up a considerable amount of floor space.

REMEMBER

■ Towel racks should be positioned within easy reach of the bath, shower, or sink.

■ Do not keep towel supplies on open shelves in a damp bathroom. Keep them dry in a closed cabinet.

■ Some everyday washing items can be used for display, but choose carefully: a new block of Provençal soap and a natural sponge are pleasing to look at, a balding back brush and fraying washcloth are not.

■ A small rack is useful for hanging out a wet bath mat to dry (see p37).

■ Keep new bars of soap in a warm closet with your towels: this scents the towels and dries out the soap, making it more long-lasting.

TOILETRIES

MOST TOILETRY ITEMS are small and oddly shaped, which means that although they do not require a large amount of space, they must be stored in an organized way. You don't need custom built-in shelves and drawers to tailor an ordinary bathroom vanity to your requirements; use small containers to group the contents for easy retrieval.

GROOMING

Bathroom procedures tend to take place at the beginning of the day, when time is limited, or at the end of the day, when light is fading. So effective organization and good lighting are essential. In a large bathroom, make provision for "wet" and "dry" grooming – toothbrushes and shaving equipment near the sink; makeup, brushes, powder, and hairdryers in a mirrored seating area.

VANITY ▷

In a compact bathroom, built-in sinks make the most effective use of space. The vanity beneath is useful for spare towels, cleaning supplies, and bulk storage of toilet paper and soaps, and the surface around the sink is a good resting place for a few small items in use, though it can quickly become cluttered.

LARGE CABINET
Shelving has been added inside the cabinet to make best use of the large space.

HIGH SHELF
Sheetrock wall hides the plumbing and provides a decorative shelf.

CONCEALED SHELVES
Shelving behind a mirrored door does not intrude on the architecture of the room.

SMALL TABLE
A table or shelf is necessary near a pedestal sink for storing items in use.

◁ PEDESTAL SINK

If you have plenty of storage space elsewhere in the room, a pedestal sink is an elegant choice. Its disadvantages are that there is not much room for storing items in daily use, and the space around the base is wasted. For a rustic look, try hanging a curtain around an old sink to create an *ad hoc* storage area that hides unsightly items.

MAKEUP ORGANIZER ▷

Different sizes of make-up containers need to be stored – a selection of various divided compartments for sorting items, as shown here, is ideal. The clear acrylic drawers allow the products on the lower layer to be retrieved quickly and easily.

■ Toiletries are usually small and therefore best suited to shallower shelves, which provide immediate visibility and easy retrieval.

■ Porous or unfinished surfaces are not recommended in bathrooms because of the danger of spillages and ring marks.

■ Easy-to-clean surfaces, such as toughened glass, tiles, and melamine-faced board, are practical and economical; other more fashionable and expensive materials, like limestone, need careful sealing.

■ Decant colorful bath salts and inexpensive bath oils into attractive glass containers.

■ Wall-mounted fittings, such as soap dishes, toothbrush holders, and towel racks, keep the basin area free of clutter.

CART
A mobile work surface is useful for wheeling accessories to different areas as needed.

△ SHAVING STAND
Though costly, a shaving stand is a good buy for devoted wet shavers; it keeps equipment together and allows ample air for drying. Never enclose a damp razor or brush; rinse the bristles from time to time in a mild borax solution.

DISPLAYING AND CONCEALING

Storage in bathrooms tends to divide between glamorous display and furtive concealment. From an ergonomic point of view, you should keep frequently used items on hand, but if that includes highly personal items, you may choose to conceal them in a cabinet. Attractively packaged cosmetics and lotions in clear or colored glass bottles inevitably take prominent positions in bathroom displays.

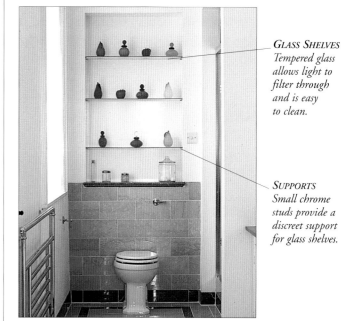

GLASS SHELVES
Tempered glass allows light to filter through and is easy to clean.

SUPPORTS
Small chrome studs provide a discreet support for glass shelves.

△ OPEN DISPLAY
The strong colors and shapes of these glass perfume bottles lend themselves to a graphically spaced display. Groups of similar objects are more attractive than a random selection of accessories.

DECORATIVE GROOVE
The MDF doors are given decorative definition.

DOOR HANDLES
Chrome fittings are well suited to a modern bathroom.

SHELVED ALCOVE
MDF-lined recess designed to store toilet paper and reading material.

△ HIDDEN FROM VIEW
Concealing the toilet tank and plumbing looks neater and provides storage space, though access must be allowed for maintenance. Shelves will usually be shallow but sufficient for most toiletries.

BATHROOM PLANS

BATHROOMS VARY TREMENDOUSLY in size and shape, but with careful planning even the most compact bathroom can provide adequate storage. Existing plumbing and water pipes often determine the placement of the sink, shower, bath, and toilet, so establish their positions before you start planning your storage. Once you have determined your storage requirements – whether you choose to house just your toiletries or to have a place for everything from soap to clothes – then you can decide whether a built-in bathroom or another style best meets your needs.

FAMILY BATHROOM

Family bathrooms must hold all things for all people – from baby's bath toys to father's shaving equipment. Where young children are concerned, safety must be considered: medicines, toiletries, and cleaning supplies should be kept high out of reach. Multi-occupancy also necessitates easy cleaning-up facilities: plenty of hooks – some at child height – for robes and towels are useful.

DESIGN POINTS

■ Storage should be site-specific: towel racks ought to be within reach of the bath or shower, and makeup near a mirror and natural light.

■ Box in plumbing above the toilet to allow for narrow shelves behind doors. If the cistern is also concealed, you must allow access to it.

■ Do not position storage for towels too close to steamy areas. For a self-indulgence, install cabinets with a heating element to keep towels warm and dry.

HOOKS ABOVE BATH
Washcloths and a net bag of toys drip-dry between use directly into the bath.

DEEP CABINET
Large cabinets are useful for storing a supply of spare towels – keep away from the bath to avoid condensation.

BUILT-IN CABINETS
Shallow shelves in a cabinet store medicines and cleaning materials out of children's reach.

RECESSED SHELVING
Toiletries and items in regular use should be kept within easy reach of the sink.

TOWEL RINGS
Chrome rings or low hooks allow children to reach for – and put away – their own towels.

VANITY
Vanities under sinks are particularly useful for bulky items, such as children's potty chairs and diapers.

SMALL BATHROOM

A small room forces you to consider your storage needs in a highly efficient way. You should restrict what you can keep in the bathroom to what is absolutely necessary, such as toiletries and grooming equipment in daily use – bulky items, like spare towels, will need to be stored elsewhere. The advantage of constricted space, however, is that it often works better ergonomically as everything is always close at hand.

TOWEL RACK
Where floor space is limited, it makes good sense to have the towel rack set at a high level.

BUILT-IN CABINET
Located above the sink, allowing space for the shelf below, the cabinet doors serve as makeup and shaving mirrors.

MARBLE SHELF
Acting as a finishing detail for the tiling, a marble shelf provides a surface for items in use.

BATH MAT RACK
Conveniently located beside the shower, a chrome rack above the radiator allows the bath mat to dry.

ACCESSORIES
A wall-mounted soap dish and toothbrush mug keep the area around the sink free from clutter.

TRADITIONAL BATHROOM

Not everyone yearns for a sleek, built-in bathroom. Some prefer the notion of a more romantic, leisurely room using old pieces of freestanding furniture that were never intended for bathroom use. You will need plenty of floor space with clearance around the various items of furniture to retain a feeling of spaciousness. In large bathrooms, always be careful not to let the luxury of space divert you from the necessary task of storing items close to where they will be used.

ARMOIRE
There is ample storage for linen and towels in an armoire.

LOW CABINET
This waist-high cabinet doubles as room divider and cosmetics storage.

DRESSING TABLE
A table with drawers acts as work surface and storage for makeup.

HOOKS
A set of hooks is practical for bathrobes and other clothing.

LAUNDRY
A large basket is useful for catching dirty clothes before bathing.

BATH RACK
Roll-edge baths have no surface for accessories: a rack across the bath addresses the problem.

TOWEL RACK
Freestanding towel racks can be moved to different positions.

BEDROOM

THE PRIME PURPOSE of a bedroom may be sleep, but where storage is concerned the bedroom is usually multifaceted, playing host to all sorts of different items from books and televisions to clothing and jewelry. It may also serve as a home office, in which case you will have to organize your storage well to allow the room to return to its domestic role at night. A spare room that is used only occasionally is convenient for storing impersonal, bulky items like luggage or sports equipment.

BEDTIME

STORAGE IS INEVITABLY focused around the bed, and its purpose is to facilitate evening and early morning activities – reading, fumbling in the dark for a glass of water, or switching off your alarm clock first thing. You need to be able to reach things easily, so a table or shelf by the bed is essential.

PERSONAL ITEMS

For reasons of privacy or security you may prefer to keep certain items, such as jewelry and medications, in close proximity to the bed. A small cabinet with shelves, or shallow drawers in a bedside table, is ideal for this purpose.

△ SMALL CABINET
A bedside cabinet or table should be able to hold a lamp, book, and glass (or tray if you enjoy breakfast in bed). Do not overcrowd, or you will knock things over in the dark.

◁ SHELVING IN THE EAVES
Sloping ceilings do not necessarily mean limited storage space. An attic bedroom can take advantage of space in the eaves for shelving and drawers. The shelves must be built in, as each shelf will vary in depth.

REMEMBER

■ Bedroom storage should include space for large, bulky items like bedding, as well as smaller possessions.

■ Allow for a variety of different storage systems for nonclothing items – shelving, drawers, and chests all have a place in the bedroom.

■ Consider what items you are likely to need near the bed before choosing the storage for this area. A shelf over or beside the bed is a good way to store books or other less personal items, but a bedside cabinet or table with drawers will allow more privacy.

BEDDING

Allow sufficient space to accommodate spare linen and out-of-season bedding. Bed linen should not be kept year after year in a warm linen closet, as it will discolor over time, so storage in the bedroom is ideal. Place cedar balls with your blankets to keep moths away.

△ BLANKET BASKET OR CHEST
Wicker baskets, chests, and trunks remain versatile and useful storage choices, particularly for bulky items like blankets. Lightweight wicker baskets can be moved easily around the room, while large, sturdy wooden chests or trunks may double as seating.

◁ PULL-OUT BAGS
Make use of otherwise wasted space under the bed. Store spare bedding here, as well as other items that are not used on a regular basis, such as out-of-season sweaters. Large, zip-up bags that protect from dust are ideal for this purpose.

CLOTHES

CLOTHES THAT ARE STORED properly look better and
last longer. There should be adequate hanging space
in closets so that the garments are well ventilated,
and shoulders and sleeves do not rub against surfaces
or get caught in the door. A combination of long and
short hanging space, shelves, and drawers is ideal.

BUILT-IN OPTIONS

Integrated clothes storage tends
to make better use of space and
is easier to tailor to your personal
requirements than freestanding
alternatives. However, built-in
storage can be expensive, and
must fit in with the proportions
and architecture of your room.

CONCEALING CURTAIN
The draping quality of the
fabric suits the decorative
style of this room.

◁ **IMPROVISED CLOSET**
Curtaining off an alcove or section of a room
to hide a clothes rod is an inexpensive way
to provide basic storage. A clothes rod on its
own is cheaper still, but does not have the
benefit of dust protection. This is probably
the most flexible of the "built-in" options,
as it is easy to dismantle.

REMEMBER

■ Contoured wooden hangers
are better for your clothes than
wire ones, which bend easily
and can catch on garments.

■ Drawers are more expensive
than shelves. Allow for
different depths of shelving.

■ Good lighting is essential
for clothes selection. For deep
closets, interior fluorescents are
useful. Consider lighting that
comes on automatically when
the door opens.

■ For seasonal storage, place
clean clothes in sealed bags
or covered boxes. Cedar balls
or shavings will deter moths.

FREESTANDING OPTIONS

A well-designed freestanding armoire can provide a striking focal point in a room, and of course can go with you if you move. However, it is rarely big enough to hold more than one person's clothes, and interior fittings tend not to be as flexible.

ARMOIRE ▷
This ornate armoire was specially designed to supplement a couple's dressing room, and so was equipped only with shelves for folded clothes and accessories such as shoes, hats, and bags. The fretwork doors are lined with fabric – a similar effect can be achieved with a grille and pleated fabric.

DOUBLE DOORS
Fabric-lined doors protect clothes inside from dust.

OUTER COVER
The cover fits neatly over the internal frame to protect the clothes.

TIE-BACKS
Fabric strips hold back the "doors" for easy access.

SHELVES
Looped at the top, fabric shelves for clothes and shoes hang from a central rod.

△ **BUILT-IN CLOSET**
Simple sliding doors glide open to reveal the inside of the closet. When closed, they form an abstract background perfectly in keeping with the architecture of the room. There is ample storage for clothes and luggage, with a narrow recess designed to hold a briefcase or bag. The shallow drawers are ideal for underwear and scarves.

◁ **WALK-IN CLOSET**
If you have the luxury of space, a walk-in closet set up like a small storage room with drawers, hanging rods, and shelves is ideal. Transparent drawers allow instant visibility for accessories, and high-level shelves can be used for out-of-season storage. An absence of windows means less exposure to dust, but lighting must be good.

HANGING SPACE

Short hanging for jackets and shirts
Long hanging for coats, long skirts, and dresses

3ft 3in (1m) *3ft 3in (1m)*
4ft 3in–4ft 11in (1.3–1.5m)

Short hanging for pants and short skirts
Extra space beneath for shoes on racks

A variety of single and double hanging makes the best use of space. A closet should be a minimum of 24in (60cm) deep to hold adult clothes.

△ **CLOTHES TENT**
Reminiscent of old "campaign" styles of furniture, several versions of these fabric armoires are available. The internal structure is a chrome or wooden frame from which to hang clothes and shelves. A canvas tent fits over the frame, with flaps at the front instead of doors.

ACCESSORIES

WHEN PLANNING YOUR BEDROOM storage, remember the array of accessories that supplement your basic wardrobe – everything from earrings to shoes. Such items often have to be stored in a specialized way to facilitate easy retrieval and offer protection. In recent years, manufacturers have designed numerous ingenious solutions specifically for the efficient storage and management of accessories.

SMALL ITEMS

It is extremely frustrating to waste precious time rummaging through crammed drawers and bags to locate small accessories such as jewelry, gloves, and underwear. Make sure that you sort and store them in a highly organized fashion. The key to successful storage of small sundries is good lighting and the ability to see everything at a glance for instant selection. Seek out small pockets of space and use the backs of doors – large cupboards and deep drawers are not appropriate for small items.

REMEMBER

■ Try to have all your accessories instantly visible – not stacked so that items at the bottom are never used. Look for the many specialized products on the market that help organize the insides of cabinets and drawers.

■ Numerous small drawers are useful for the organization of accessories. It is crucial that the depth of drawer be exactly right, so that you do not have to dig for your belongings.

■ An inexpensive way of protecting shoes is to keep them in their original boxes. Cut a window at the end for easy identification, or attach a Polaroid portrait of the contents of each box.

■ Try to keep pairs of objects together so that you do not have to search for the missing item every time.

△ TIE RACKS
Various types of tie rack are available that either hang from the clothes rod inside the closet or, to save space, on the back of a door, as shown above. All prevent ties from becoming creased.

△ JEWELRY BOARD
An improvised system of pins and tape on a wall-mounted, felt-covered board prevents jewelry from becoming tangled, keeps pairs of earrings together, and offers instant visibility.

ACCESSORIES RACK ▷
Gloves rival socks in their ability to lose their partners. This system of pins and small pouches looped over a rack keeps gloves in pairs and scarves together for easy retrieval.

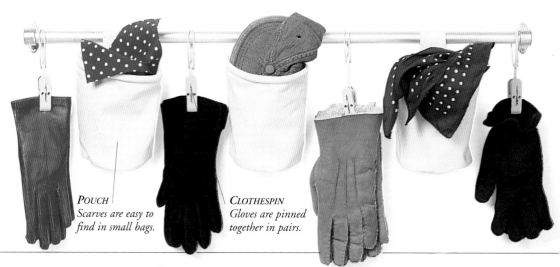

POUCH
Scarves are easy to find in small bags.

CLOTHESPIN
Gloves are pinned together in pairs.

DRAWER ORGANIZER ▷
A creative solution to the problem
of chaotic underwear drawers, this
expandable plastic drawer insert
separates and sorts underwear,
socks, and scarves. The entire
contents of the drawer are visible at
a glance, so you are more likely to
use the items on a frequent basis.

▽ **BUILT-IN SOLUTION**
Extra storage is squeezed out of a
small bedroom by framing the door
with a selection of different-sized
cabinets and numerous narrow
drawers. Small drawers are ideal
for storing accessories like scarves,
underwear, and hosiery.

ADJUSTABLE INSERTS
*Rows of dividers clip together
and can be cut to fit snugly
inside the drawer.*

SHOES

Most people have many pairs of shoes,
from everyday footwear to shoes worn only
occasionally. They are often kept at the
bottom of a closet, where they take up
considerable space and tend to collect dust.
Consider these other options.

△ **SHOE CABINET**
Specially designed deep drawers with metal rods are
ideal for storing shoes. To extend the life of good
leather shoes, protect them from dust and keep
them spaced apart so that they are not touching;
shoe trees ensure they keep their shape.

DOOR HOOKS
*Three metal
hooks attach the
fabric shoe
pockets to the
back of a door.*

SHOE POUCHES
*Small pockets
separate and
protect shoes from
rubbing against
one another.*

△ **FABRIC POCKETS**
A space-saving shoe organizer that hangs on the back
of a door can store a large number of indoor shoes
and accessories, but is less practical for heavily used
outdoor shoes, which will quickly soil the fabric.

BEDROOM PLANS

SLEEPING MAKES VERY LITTLE demand on storage capacity, so it is well worth exploiting the bedroom as much as possible for other purposes. Although it was considered unhygienic by many in the early twentieth century to keep clothes in the bedroom – "It is not a clean thing to do, and makes the room horribly untidy," opined the French architect Le Corbusier – for most people today it is often the only option. There is no doubt that a dressing room or walk-in closet is ideal, but because the space for these is often carved out of an existing bedroom, you do have to be careful not to ruin the room's proportions.

BEDROOM WITH DRESSING ROOM

A separate dressing room reduces the pressure for storage in the bedroom itself, so that the sleeping area stays reasonably uncluttered. It also allows for one partner to dress without disturbing the other. Unlike a walk-in closet, a dressing room should ideally have natural light, a mirror for grooming, and sufficient space in which to dress. A door to the room is not necessary, as the clothes are protected behind the closet fronts.

CLOTHES DRAWERS
A chest of small and shallow drawers divides closet territory and is useful for underwear and accessories.

HIGH CABINETS
Areas that are difficult to access can be used for medium-term storage of out-of-season clothes.

WINDOW
A window to the side provides welcome natural light in a dressing room.

CHEST OF DRAWERS
Useful for small items and as a surface for personal display, a chest of drawers also gives focus to the room.

BUILT-IN CLOSET
Segregated hanging space is provided by built-in closets on either side of the mirror.

DOORWAY
An open doorway leading into the dressing room provides a feeling of spaciousness, and the wall offers extra storage space.

BEDSIDE TABLE
Positioned on either side of the bed, a table is needed for books and other bedside items.

BEDROOM WITH WALK-IN CLOSET

A walk-in closet is the most efficient way to store clothes, since there are no doors once you are inside, and you can see everything at a glance. Because the garments need to be kept free from dust, a walk-in closet must have a main door and preferably no windows. Ideally, each partner should have a closet, tailored to his or her specific needs.

OPEN HANGING BAR
Clothes are accessible and easily retrievable in this dust-free environment.

SHELVING
Adjustable shelves, as well as drawers, accommodate sweaters and T-shirts.

BEDSIDE SHELF
A custom-built shelf eliminates the need for a bedside table.

SHOE RACK
Angled racks along the bottom of the closet make shoes easily visible.

WOODEN CHEST
A chest or ottoman at the end of the bed stores spare blankets and doubles as a seat.

SLIDING DOOR
A door that slides back is space-effective, as it does not obscure clothes or hinder circulation.

SMALL BEDROOM

For ingenious, space-saving ideas for a small bedroom, look to a ship's cabin, which is always designed with plenty of built-in cabinets and shelving. Building in storage around the doorway is particularly effective, as is making use of space under and around the bed. Care must be taken, however, to leave sufficient clearance space around the furniture for dressing and undressing.

HIGH CABINET
A built-in cabinet makes use of "dead" ceiling space above a doorway.

HANGING SPACE
Two-level hanging is particularly appropriate for men's clothes, and economizes on space.

BEDSIDE SHELVING
The lower shelves act as a bedside table, while the higher ones give extra display space.

OPEN SHELVING
The shelves form a small lobby, with plenty of space for books and other collectibles.

UNDER THE BED
A custom-made base with shallow drawers for spare bedding makes good use of otherwise wasted space.

CHILD'S ROOM

FROM THE FANTASY PLAY of early childhood to the decorative self-expression of the teenage years, a child's bedroom is her stronghold, a refuge from adult intrusion. Imagination is a vital ingredient of children's play and learning, but do not confuse creativity with chaos: neat, well-organized areas for toys and games as well as for reading and study are liberating, not restricting. If your children share a bedroom, it may have to accommodate differing work, play, and sleep requirements. Storage must be flexible and varied to meet the family's evolving needs.

CLOTHING

CHILDREN'S CLOTHING REQUIREMENTS change significantly over the years – from the soft sleepers of babyhood to the piles of T-shirts and jeans favored by teenagers. Child-sized furniture is compact, but not a good buy for those of us on budgets, since it has a limited lifespan. A standard-sized chest of drawers, however, will last from babyhood to adulthood.

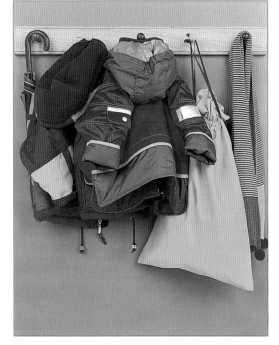

HANGING CLOTHES

For the first few years of a child's life, minimal hanging space is sufficient. As the child grows, dresses, coats, jackets, and blouses make more demands on closet space. Adult clothes rods can be adapted or doubled for children's use.

◁ PEG BOARD

Pegs at a low height are very easy to use. They can be highly decorative and, in the early years when hanging needs are few, they are good for displaying items of clothing in frequent use.

HANGING BAR ▷

This adjustable extension rod is useful for adding children's hanging space to the short hanging rod in an adult's closet. Alternatively, it can be used in a small closet to provide double-hanging space at child-sized height.

FOLDED CLOTHES

Most children's clothes are better off folded than hanging. Ordinary chests of drawers are good for babies and teenagers, but are not ideal in the middle years when children tend to stuff clothes in and use only the top layer. Folded clothes should not be stacked too high, as shelves will inevitably become extremely untidy.

◁ CLOSET SPACE

An attic closet offers shelves and a large drawer, as well as a niche for spare bedding for friends' overnight stays. The fluorescent lighting strip above the door allows easy selection of garments.

WIRE BASKETS ▷

This stack of baskets is an inexpensive substitute for a chest of drawers. The system is flexible and adjustable, and allows the child to see the contents at a glance.

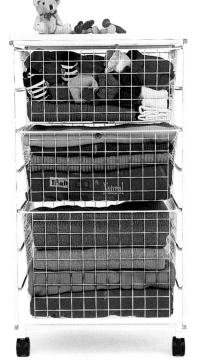

REMEMBER

■ Cleaning up does not come naturally. To encourage children to put away their clothes, design storage that they can reach, and be inventive: use colorful pegs and amusing clothes hangers, for example.

■ Avoid too many deep drawers: they will quickly become messy. Shallow ones are easier to keep in order.

■ Outfit chests of drawers with safety catches to prevent young children from pulling them out on top of themselves.

■ A rod attached to the underside of a shelf can be used for hanging clothes.

WORK AND PLAY

OVER THE YEARS, storage must adapt and grow with the child to accommodate a variety of different functions. Floor space is important for children up to the age of about ten – after that they will be more oriented toward desk or tabletop activities. Storage should be organized to ease and simplify the unpopular task of cleaning up.

TOYS AND GAMES

Display is an essential ingredient of storage for children – what the eye doesn't see, the hand doesn't play with. For this reason, shelves are better than cupboards, but it is good to have a variety of methods, including baskets and drawers, to adapt to the changing requirements of the growing child.

CHILDREN'S SHELVING

12in (30cm) deep for books and valuables

18in (45cm) deep for crates and larger toys

A mixture of deep shelves at a low height for play and shallow shelving out of reach is ideal, especially in a shared bedroom.

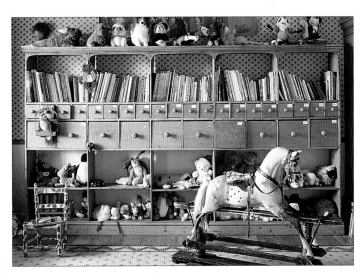

HIGH SHELF
Keep fragile toys and old books on a top shelf so that they are on display but are not damaged.

REMEMBER

■ Toys for younger children should be at a low level to encourage play, but be sure that potentially hazardous toys and small pieces are out of the reach of babies and toddlers.

■ Do not display toys all at once: put some away and rotate them periodically so that they do not lose their novelty value.

■ Old-fashioned toy boxes look pretty, but their depth makes locating toys difficult, and their heavy lids can trap tiny fingers.

■ Allow for a variety of storage systems to accommodate everything from bulky toys and large books to small blocks and tiny plastic play people.

△ TOY STORAGE
Junk shops make good hunting grounds for versatile pieces like this old pine unit, which acts almost as a toy filing system. It has plenty of space for books, display shelves at different heights for stuffed toys, and drawers of varying sizes – some labeled – for special treasures.

SHELVING
The system is adjustable, so the shelves can be raised and lowered as required.

HIGH BED ▷
In a small room, a bed with storage – in this case, adjustable shelving – and/or a study area underneath provides the best use of floor space, and gives the sense of enclosure and privacy that becomes more of a priority as the child gets older.

HAMMOCK ▷
Stuffed toys harbor
dust, which can trigger
asthma in vulnerable
children, but it is hard to banish
them entirely – a hammock keeps
them suspended within view.

BOOK BASKET
High beds do not have the
advantage of bedside tables, so
attach a side basket for books.

PAINT TRAY
Set paint pots
into a sponge-
lined tray to
hold them firm.

SMALL DRAWERS
Keep collections
of tiny objects in
small drawers.

PLASTIC CRATES
Transparent boxes
obviate the need
for labels.

MOBILE UNIT
Crates on casters
transport blocks
around the room.

TEENAGERS' BELONGINGS

Untidiness seems to be an essential element of adolescence, but a teenager is more likely to clean up if provided with stylish and easy-to-use storage. Before investing in expensive units, however, brace yourself to seeing them "customized" by their teenage owners.

△ **STORAGE CUBES**
A full wall of units specially designed for a teenager provides storage for many objects, including a television and a selection of open display shelves. The various compartments open in different ways as their doors are hinged at the side, top, and bottom.

△ **STUDY AREA**
A quiet place to study is essential for older children. This room for a teenage student makes use of a top-lit alcove, benefiting from the view and natural light. In the pedestal unit, brightly colored boxes on open shelves and drawers are ideal for storing possessions.

CHILD'S ROOM PLANS

CHILDREN ARE OFTEN ALLOCATED small, irregularly shaped rooms that no one else wants. However, unless you have the luxury of a separate playroom, consider sacrificing a larger room for younger children to share, providing them with plenty of floor space for play, then moving them to smaller rooms when they are older. Children's storage should be flexible to accommodate their changing needs – modular furniture is ideal. Take care not to fill every nook and cranny with fixed storage: for young children, idiosyncratic spaces are important areas for pretend play.

NURSERY

Comfort, practicality, and, above all, safety are essential in a nursery. A baby will spend a considerable amount of time high up on a changing pad, and cannot be left alone, so this area in particular must be well planned, with all the equipment you need close at hand. Too much freestanding furniture will obstruct the floor space when the baby is mobile, but sturdy, adjustable shelves for toys can be used later for books and games.

DESIGN POINTS

■ Choose an adjustable shelving system that allows brackets to be securely attached to the shelves for stability. Freestanding furniture should be bolted to the wall so that small children cannot pull it down on top of them.

■ Position low shelves to be accessible, but not so low that children decide to use them as jungle gyms.

■ If possible, place furniture away from windows so a child is not tempted to climb up. Use safety locks to prevent accidents.

HANGING TOY ORGANIZER
Fabric pockets provide overflow accommodation for stuffed toys and are a decorative wall feature.

SEATING AREA
A comfortable window seat for an adult or older child also provides useful storage space beneath for toys.

CHANGING AREA
For safety reasons, diapers, wipes, and creams must be kept within easy reach of the pad.

WICKER BASKET
A large basket or box is useful for a quick clean-up of toys before bedtime.

UNDER THE CRIB
Make use of the space beneath the crib to accommodate extra boxes for toys or accessories.

ADJUSTABLE SHELVING
Shelf or drawer space is required for babies' tiny clothes; hanging space is not yet necessary.

SHARED ROOM

A room of their own is not a priority for most children under the age of ten – younger children often prefer company. As they get older, however, sharing a room can lead to tensions if the space is not planned to give each sibling some sense of their own "territory." Bunk beds may be the answer; otherwise, shelves or a screen can act as a partition between two beds. Allocate shelf and closet space, and separate bulletin boards on which they can express themselves individually.

FLEXIBLE SHELVING
Adjustable shelves allow for the changing needs of growing children, from toys to stereo systems.

HIGH SHELVES
An older child will appreciate a shelf to keep precious possessions out of a young sibling's grasp.

CABINET SPACE
Easily accessible cabinets provide a place for toys and games.

DESK AREA
A quiet study area, and somewhere to house a computer, is desirable for an older child.

PARTITION SHELVING
A chest with shelves and drawers doubles as a bedside table and room divider.

STUDY AREA
A large desk with shelves and drawers will accommodate a computer, books, and stationery.

STEREO NICHE
Positioned close by, the stereo can be controlled from the desk.

TELEVISION ALCOVE
The television is viewed from the bed – the alcove should have an outlet and reception facilities.

LARGE DRAWERS
Privacy is a priority for many teenagers, so try to provide adequate drawer space.

CLOSETS
Allow plenty of closet space for expanding collections of clothes.

TEENAGER'S ROOM

Teenagers generally need as much independence as is feasible in a family household. A room at the extremities of the house, such as an attic or basement, which allows full-volume music, is ideal. Children generally enjoy displaying their possessions on open shelves, while teenagers are likely to prefer more privacy in the form of drawers and cabinets. It is essential to include a clearly defined, well-organized area for study in a teenager's room.

LOW HANGING
Sloping ceilings mean that hanging space is restricted to jackets and pants.

HOME OFFICE

ADVANCES IN TECHNOLOGY and changes in working practices have resulted in more people than ever working from home. This does not mean that you have to re-create a commercial office at home – instead, it is an opportunity to create a working environment personally tailored to your storage needs, without having to consider the dictates of others. You can project an individual look, by using baskets instead of filing trays, for example, but at the same time you need to retain some visual division between work and domestic life to protect your professional credibility.

PART-TIME OFFICE

IF YOU DO NOT HAVE the luxury of a whole room at your disposal for a home office, you may have to squeeze two functions into one room. The benefit of allocating a precise area to work, rather than migrating to wherever there is space, is that you have a permanent place to house your papers without the risk of loss or damage.

REMEMBER

■ Home offices can quickly become messy, and allowing your working life to intrude on domestic life can destroy the idea of home as a haven. If you are working in an open-plan room, partition shelving or a floor-to-ceiling curtain or blind will conceal the clutter and provide a sense of privacy.

■ Keep your papers and office equipment where they will not be disturbed by others. The better the storage facilities, the easier this will be.

■ Allow sufficient electrical outlets for all of your office equipment. Keep computers on a stable surface, out of direct sunlight, with plenty of ventilation around them.

CONCEALED OFFICES

When working from home, it is essential to delineate between office and domestic life. If you work part-time or are restricted in space, efficient storage becomes even more important for putting away work when your office space has to return to "home" mode.

△ **CORNER CUPBOARD**
It is often possible to carve out a space from an existing room to form an office alcove. Here, a corner hung with shelves, easily shut away behind decorative doors, serves as a mini office.

◁ **WORK STATION**
Some furniture manufacturers are now producing units especially for home offices, designed to hold a computer and serve filing needs. This compact unit folds neatly together to hide its contents and converts into an unobtrusive cabinet.

△ **KITCHEN WORK SPACE**
Borrowed space on the kitchen table, plus some pigeonholes, shelves, and good task lighting, is often all that is required to enable you to deal in a reasonably orderly fashion with correspondence, bills, and household affairs.

TEMPORARY OFFICES

Even if it is only to sort out domestic bills and correspondence, allocate a place in the home – whether it is a bureau in the living room or a corner in the kitchen – for household paperwork and stationery.

ORGANIZER
Hanging files fold up and convert into a portable case.

COLORFUL BOXES
Fabric-covered boxes do not look out of place in a domestic setting.

DOCUMENT SAFE
Important papers are secure in a lockable, fireproof box.

FOLD-AWAY OFFICE ▷
If space is restricted, an office that can be dismantled easily is a good option, as it may be stored in a closet. This "office" consists of a collapsible table and chair and portable filing systems.

FULL-TIME OFFICE

HOME OFFICES should be planned carefully from the outset. You need to assess how much space you will require, and design storage around your *modus operandi*. A well-planned and organized office is especially important if you plan to see clients and colleagues in your working area.

WORKING

In order to work most effectively, your office must be designed in a way that facilitates your working habits, just as to be able to cook efficiently you need an ergonomically planned kitchen. Your desk is the nucleus around which storage must be organized. You should not have to leave your chair to reach frequently needed items.

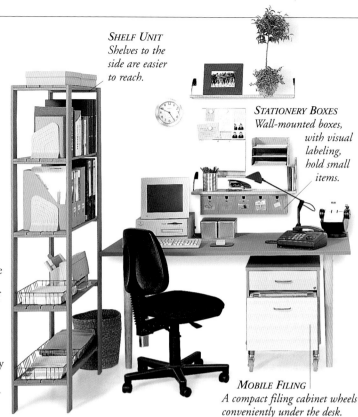

SHELF UNIT
Shelves to the side are easier to reach.

STATIONERY BOXES
Wall-mounted boxes, with visual labeling, hold small items.

BASIC DESK ▷
The simplest table can be accessorized to provide adequate storage facilities. Keep the surface of the desk as clear as possible: have freestanding and wall-mounted shelving within easy reach, and use a good filing cabinet.

MOBILE FILING
A compact filing cabinet wheels conveniently under the desk.

HIGH-TECH OFFICE ▷
New technology, though it was supposed to simplify office life, makes its own demands on space. Different professions have their own particular storage needs – in this office, solid shelving has been designed specifically to take videocassettes, stereo components, monitors, and other related equipment. If you have the space, it is desirable to divide your office into clearly defined areas for different tasks. A small refrigerator and snack area avoid disruptive visits to the main kitchen.

△ STUDY AREA
Not all occupations demand high-powered technological equipment. Here, an elegant desk sets a calm and reflective pace for thoughtful work. Although antique, its collection of drawers of differing sizes and numerous recesses are useful in a modern setting for accommodating paperwork and stationery items.

REMEMBER

■ Before investing in filing cabinets, establish the size of paper you intend to store. Some systems are designed for letter-sized paper, others for legal size.

■ Periodically review what paperwork should be kept, and move documents that are not current but must be retained to "dead" storage areas.

■ If desk space is limited, consider wall-mounted filing trays or baskets that clip on underneath a shelf.

■ Pens and pencils can be kept in a simple tin can, or a decorative mug. Use stationery dividers in drawers to organize small items.

SORTING AND FILING

The arrival of the computer was supposed to herald the dawn of the "paperless office," but it has rarely turned out so in practice. Paperwork has a tendency to accumulate at a great rate, and though most people find it difficult to throw anything away, a degree of discipline is essential if you are to work in a small place.

◁ **FILING ROOM**
If your filing demands are heavy, and you have the space, a whole room devoted to filing, leaving your main working space clear, is ideal. Shelves should be designed to fit the depth of magazine or box files, and good lighting is essential.

STEPLADDER
A set of steps allows access to the top shelves.

△ **PAPER FILING**
Bulldog clips pinned to a wall are an effective visual reminder for bills to be paid. Lever arch box files are useful for papers that are no longer relevant but need to be kept, while fan-style files suit current documents.

FILING BASKETS ▷
If it is not paper but irregularly shaped objects that you need to file, baskets may provide the ideal storage medium. Housed in recesses, these identical baskets look informal and stylish, but they are also a very efficient sorting system.

LABELS
Simple, handwritten package labels identifying the contents are attached to the handles.

DESK SHELVING

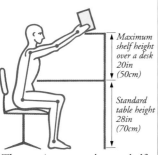

Maximum shelf height over a desk 20in (50cm)

Standard table height 28in (70cm)

The maximum reach to a shelf above a desk from a sitting position is 20in (50cm), but this does not take into account reaching over large equipment, such as computers.

HOME OFFICE PLANS

ALL TOO OFTEN, THE HOME OFFICE has to make do with the space that remains after the bedrooms and living rooms have been allocated. If your work is full-time, however, your office should not be left as an afterthought. You may need to change the dynamics of the house – perhaps your children could share a bedroom – in order to free up a room for your office. Whatever its size, your work space must always be carefully planned and efficient, with plenty of storage close at hand and enough clearance around the furniture for comfort.

PROFESSIONAL OFFICE

If you need to present a strong professional front at home, your office space must be a priority. The office should be located so that visitors do not have to tour through your house, with your domestic life clearly visible, in order to reach it. In a large office, in which several people may work at once, try to break down the space into separate zones such as reception, work, meeting, library, and filing areas. This will mean greater efficiency and less disruption to others.

DESIGN POINTS

■ An L-shape plan consisting of your desk and shelving maximizes your reach from a seated position.

■ Allow plenty of space for files, catalogs, and reference material, and plan for expansion. As a rule of thumb, allocate approximately 50 percent more storage space than you currently require.

■ You will need 39in (1m) clearance in front of a filing cabinet for easy access to drawers, and 35in (90cm) in front of shelving.

SUPPLY CLOSET
Adjustable shelving, open or in a large cabinet, is ideal for storing paper, envelopes, and files.

FLAT FILE
An architect's flat file is useful in any office where large sheets of paper need to be kept flat.

FILING CABINET
A low cabinet demarcates two separate work areas and provides a surface for items in use.

REFRESHMENT AREA
Trips to the domestic kitchen can be avoided if there is a coffee-making area in the room.

OPEN SHELVING
Sturdy MDF is well suited to the storage of large, heavy files and catalogs.

ROOM DIVIDER
In addition to housing lateral files, a cube storage system also provides an element of privacy for the meeting area.

SMALL OFFICE

Restricted office space has the advantage of enforced efficiency. It should be planned with utmost precision, and storage must earn its keep. As with a galley kitchen, a line of cabinets along either side of a small room is ergonomic, as everything is close at hand. Because much of the floor space is taken up by desks, you will be more dependent on desk drawers and wall-mounted shelves rather than freestanding units for storage.

WALL-MOUNTED SHELVING
Sturdy shelves, within reach of the desk, are useful for files and attaching work lights.

COMPUTER STAND
Keeping the computer on a special swivel-arm stand frees up the desk for other activities.

PULL-OUT KEYBOARD
A pull-out shelf allows the keyboard to be concealed under the desk when not in use.

PEDESTAL CABINETS
A set of drawers at either end of the desk double as a support for the tabletop.

RECYCLING CONTAINER
Place a large box close to the printer for waste paper.

DUAL-PURPOSE ROOM

Sharing space – most commonly with the guest room or dining room – is often the only option for an office in a small house or apartment. This can be successful, provided you plan it carefully so that the two functions do not intrude on each other. You will need plenty of storage, as tidiness and order are crucial in a shared space. Select flexible furniture such as movable cabinets, which enable you to wheel office items away when you need the room for domestic use. A corner arrangement helps keep the office layout as unobtrusive as possible.

L-SHAPED DESK
An L-shape offers the most compact way of working, with good access to a wide area.

PARTITION SHELVING
Freestanding shelving can give a perceived sense of territorial boundries.

STORAGE UNIT
A compact, ready-made unit that offers open shelving and some concealment of unsightly equipment is ideal.

SOFABED
Look for dual-purpose furniture: a sofabed provides comfortable seating in the office and a space-saving bed.

MOBILE TABLE
A table on casters can be wheeled away if inconvenient.

OTHER SPACES

WHEN LOOKING AROUND a potential new home, we tend to focus all our attention on the kitchen and living spaces, ignoring the less glamorous ancillary areas such as utility rooms, basements, and attics. These functional rooms, however, are the very

backbone of the house, the hard-working spaces that allow the other rooms to remain gracious and uncluttered. You should outfit the ancillary areas as soon as you can: planned to reap maximum efficiency, they are your most valuable storage assets.

ATTIC AND BASEMENT

THESE TWO SPACES at the extremes of the house are often inefficiently used. They tend to be filled with junk that should have been disposed of long ago. Insulate the attic and waterproof the basement to maximize storage opportunities. Improving accessibility will also help: good lighting, strong flooring, and safe access are essential.

◁ **ATTIC STORAGE**
Hidden from view, an attic does not need sophisticated storage. However, order is essential for it not to degenerate into a jumble and to make the best use of space. Here, shipping crates stacked on their sides create a rudimentary modular storage system.

WOODEN CRATES
Crates turned on their sides make contents more easily accessible.

UNDERGROUND WINE STORAGE ▷
A prefabricated concrete wine cellar can be installed in houses without a basement, provided there is space to excavate several yards deep. Entrance is via a trap-door, and the bottles are stored in honeycomb modules.

REMEMBER

■ Before moving possessions to an attic or basement, consider whether you are really likely to have a use for them again. If not, dispose of them.

■ Basements provide optimum conditions for wine, but other items, such as textiles, books, and papers, will deteriorate in a damp environment. Attics are usually dry, but insulation is necessary to avoid temperature extremes.

■ Keep an inventory of items stored so that you will know where to retrieve them.

ATTIC PLAN

Outfitting your attic to take spillover of household storage is often more useful – and certainly less expensive – than converting it into an extra room. The space under the roof is ideal for long-term storage, but it can get very dusty, so contents should be properly protected.

CHEST OF DRAWERS
Furniture no longer deemed suitable to grace living areas provides useful storage for small items.

CABINETS
Flush doors along one wall conceal deep cabinets with permanent shelving.

CLOTHES PROTECTORS
Lightweight hanging closets protect out-of-season clothes from dust; moth repellent is essential.

SHELVING
Capitalize on wasted space under the eaves by putting up simple, sturdy shelves.

HALL, STAIRS, AND LANDINGS

BRIDGING PUBLIC SPACE and domestic privacy, the hall is an important place of first impressions. As a main thoroughfare, it must be designed to take a considerable amount of traffic and to provide for people discarding coats, keys, and various other items. Stairs and landings are primarily circulation spaces, but they may also offer extra storage opportunities.

◁ HAT STAND
A freestanding hat stand, though more space-consuming than wall hooks, is better for wet outdoor clothing since it allows air circulation.

STAIR CLOSETS ▷
Here, spectacular use has been made of "dead" space under the stairs by installing pull-out shelving units, thus exploiting the potential of even the tightest corner.

TOP LEVEL
High cabinets house "dead" storage, such as suitcases.

LARGE CABINETS
Detailed to look like several small cabinets, large doors conceal the boiler and coats.

SMALL CABINETS
Household maintenance items and tools are stored in a small, lockable cabinet.

ALCOVE
An alcove for display also provides an essential surface near the front door for keys and mail.

SPATIAL ILLUSION ▷
In a narrow entrance hall, a formal row of concealed cabinets can give the impression of the space being more generous than it actually is. The eye is caught by the detailing on the doors, which distracts from the real scale of the area.

HIDDEN DOORS ▷
Every house or apartment has its share of unsightly elements to conceal, whether it is the boiler or the gas meter. The owner of this house commissioned an artist to paint the staircase walls leading to the basement, making a feature of the meter cabinet.

CONCEALMENT
Curtains screen off the landing to form a private antechamber with hidden seating.

PADDED SEAT
The seat lifts up to provide extra storage underneath for bulky items, such as blankets.

◁ WINDOW SEAT
Landings are usually the most unused spaces in a house. This one, however, was spacious enough to create a curtained seating area under the window. A window seat acts as a strong focal point on a landing and provides useful storage in an otherwise "dead" space.

REMEMBER

■ Storage on stairs is restricted by fire regulations: new constructions must meet the appropriate building codes.

■ Halls accumulate a lot of clutter. You need somewhere near the front door, such as a shelf or bench, to store mail and keys. Coats, hats, shoes, and umbrellas must be tidied away, but remain accessible.

■ A set of hooks at a low level encourages children to hang up their own coats. Consider racks for muddy shoes.

UMBRELLA STAND
A tall garbage can or umbrella stand keeps water from dripping onto the hall floor.

CONSOLE
A shelf by the door acts as repository for keys and mail.

COAT HOOKS
Everyday coats may be hung on hooks rather than in the closet.

LANDING SEAT
A box offers storage and seating. If on the stairs, it must be fire resistant.

COAT CLOSET
Outdoor clothing and accessories are ideally stored in a large, well-lit coat closet by the door.

HALL, STAIRS, AND LANDINGS PLAN
If you are fortunate enough to have a spacious hall, you should be able to keep it fairly uncluttered. Narrow halls may present a problem, but with judicious planning, even cramped areas can yield extra storage space. You must always find room for coats, keys, and mail, but try to avoid too many freestanding solutions, which may impede flow.

CABINET
An understairs cabinet is a convenient place to store bulky items, such as a vacuum cleaner.

UTILITY AREAS

A ROOM DEVOTED to the practicalities of living – laundry, household maintenance, and tools – is a great luxury, as it frees up storage space in other rooms. If you do not have a utility room, you will need to allocate a place for storage, perhaps in a kitchen closet or a corner of the garage.

▽ WORKSHOP

Your tools and equipment should always be stored in a well-organized way so they are easy to find when you need them. Tool storage must be in a dry place, to avoid rusting. Keep most frequently used items at eye level, and group tools according to function.

OUTLINES
Tracing around tools on a peg board ensures you put them back in the right place.

STACKABLE TINS
Storage boxes that stack are preferable to a motley collection of jars and cans.

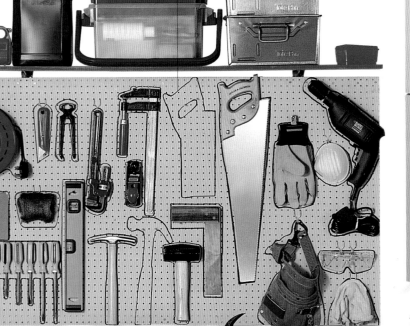

△ BROOM CLOSET

Where there is no utility room, a tall cabinet can take the bulk of cleaning equipment. Special fittings allow for storage of vacuum cleaner attachments.

LOCKABLE BOX
Toxic and flammable materials should be kept in a lockable metal box, or out of the reach of children.

POCKETS
Compartments sort frequently used tools so they are readily accessible.

△ PORTABLE TOOLS

If you do not have the space for a workshop, a portable bag loaded up with a basic set of maintenance tools saves time and space. It is also useful for transporting tools from storage to the job at hand.

FOLDAWAY BOARD
Ironing boards are cumbersome: this device folds neatly away in a cabinet.

VENETIAN BLIND
A large Venetian blind pulls down to conceal unsightly clutter.

WALL-MOUNTED DRYER
Where floor space is at a premium, consider a dryer attached to the wall.

◁ **UTILITY ROOM**
Though it is, of course, possible to store cleaning materials and laundry facilities in the kitchen or bathroom, a separate utility room is highly desirable, particularly since the range of machines that replace human toil is constantly expanding. For safety reasons, too, it is best to keep certain equipment, such as hot irons and toxic cleaning solutions, in a separate room, away from children and pets.

REMEMBER

■ It is worth losing some living space for the benefit of a utility room, because it takes the pressure off other rooms such as the kitchen, bathroom, or hall, which would otherwise need to be used for storage of cleaning and maintenance equipment.

■ Maximize closet space for cleaning equipment: attach clips and hooks to walls and the backs of doors for hanging up brooms, mops, dustpans, and vacuum cleaner attachments.

■ Wipe infrequently used tools after use with a lightly oiled rag to prevent rust. In case of accidents, keep a first-aid kit within reach of your workbench.

UTILITY ROOM PLAN

A well-planned utility room minimizes the drudgery of household tasks. Since aesthetics are not a prime consideration here, channel your resources into laying out the room for maximum efficiency. If you are planning the space from scratch, bear in mind that utility rooms are particularly useful if they can double up as a "decompression zone" with the outside world – a place to keep muddy boots or sports equipment.

RECYCLING BINS
Stackable recycling bins are practical for sorting waste, such as bottles and cans.

CLOTHES RACK
Operated by a pulley system and located over the sink, a rack allows clothes to drip dry.

CABINET
This custom-made cabinet includes a pull-out for cleaning materials.

WICKER BASKET
Dry clothes for ironing may be kept in a wicker basket; wet clothes are better in a plastic container.

STACKABLE MACHINES
Special front-loading washers and dryers can be stacked to save floor space.

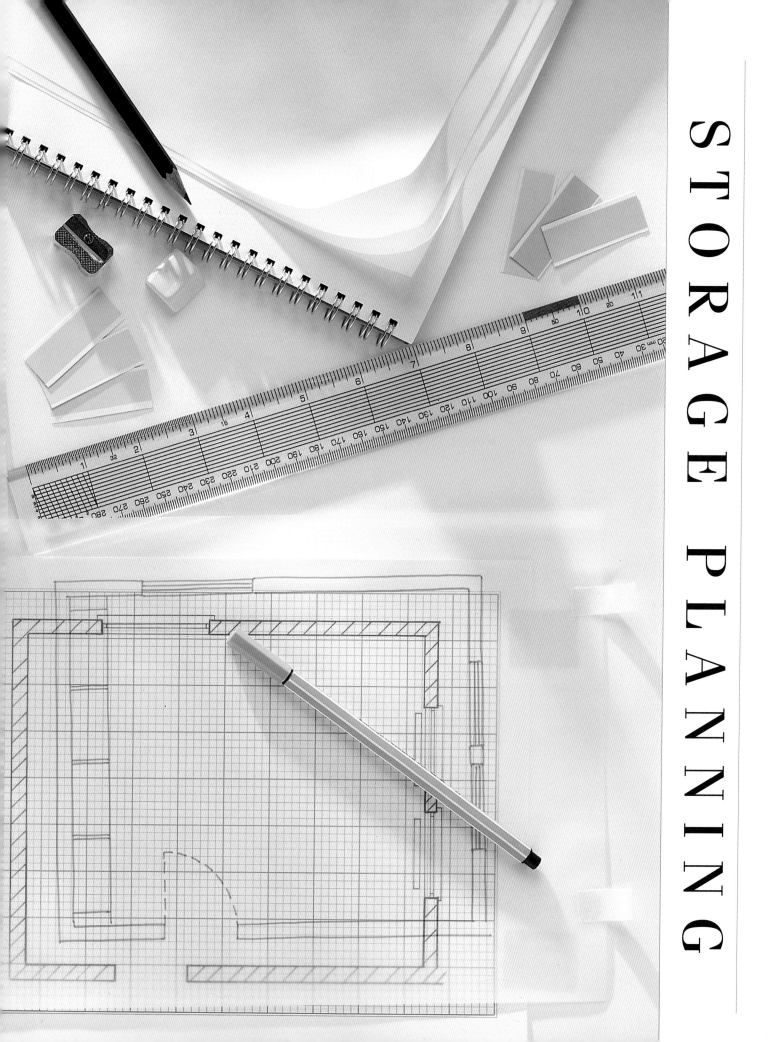

STORAGE PLANNING

DESIGN OPTIONS

BEFORE EMBARKING upon the design and planning of your
storage, consider in depth the pros and cons of each type, both
from an aesthetic and a functional point of view. There is often
more than one solution available, which is why it is necessary to
clarify your goals at the outset and then test them against each
option. Establish exactly what you need to store in each room,
then start to rule out certain practical options on aesthetic
grounds. Shelves are cost effective to build yourself, but when
drawers and cabinets are required, ready-made systems offer
better value. Stock cabinets may look out of place in a
Victorian living room, whereas well-designed built-in shelves
that respect the house's architectural details could be ideal.

POINTS TO CONSIDER

■ Bear in mind the cost of different storage
methods, but also consider durability
and flexibility as well as price. The
obvious advantage of freestanding
storage is that it can move with
you, but a good built-in solution
may well add value to your home.

■ Analyze the specific physical
attributes, such as architecture,
of the room in which you are
going to store items, and consider
how best to complement these
features in your storage plans.

■ When selecting shelving, decide on the look
you wish to create: enclosed shelves, which
require the support of side walls, give
an established, integrated feel to a
room; individual shelves, which are
supported by brackets alone, may
provide a sense of lightness,
particularly when made of glass.

■ If you are opting for portable
storage, remember that the
containers themselves will need
to be stored somewhere. Stacking
them on the floor is not practical.

FREESTANDING PIECES

A family heirloom, a rehabilitated junk-
shop find, or a beautiful modern piece
may enhance a room, while providing
useful storage for possessions. An old
decorative armoire, equipped with
shelves, is at home in any room.

ADVANTAGES
• Give focus to the room.
• Flexible; can be moved.
• Can set style of the room.

DISADVANTAGES
• Can be bulky and space-consuming.
• May take up a lot of wall space.
• Antiques may not accommodate modern needs.

BUILT-IN FURNITURE

Integrated furniture may take advantage
of existing architectural features, such as
doorways, alcoves, or long, straight runs
along walls. If a room is large enough,
consider building a false wall to
accommodate built-in shelving.

ADVANTAGES
• Can be designed to individual specification.
• Provides an acoustic buffer to other rooms.
• Possible to accommodate built-in lighting.

DISADVANTAGES
• Disruptive and often costly to build.
• Cannot be moved when you do.
• Needs careful design to fit in with architecture.

WALL-MOUNTED UNITS

The Shakers were famous for making good use of wall-mounted cabinets. While these were wooden and informal in style, modern designs of wall-mounted cabinets and shelving units are available in a wide variety of styles.

ADVANTAGES
• Practical where floor space is limited.
• Flexible in terms of positioning in the room.
• Can be taken with you if you move.

DISADVANTAGES
• Restricted in size because of wall support.
• Cabinets tend to be shallow.
• Need secure anchoring and good, strong walls.

DUAL-PURPOSE STORAGE

Furniture that doubles as storage is particularly useful where space is restricted, such as in a narrow hall or on a landing. A decorative ottoman, window seat, or bench will hold a large amount of clutter.

ADVANTAGES
• Dual function makes good use of space.
• Ideal for bulky or awkward items.
• Fits in with decorative scheme.

DISADVANTAGES
• Not practical for frequently used items.
• Other function may make access difficult.
• Storage at low level – retrieval requires bending.

PORTABLE ITEMS

Certain small objects lend themselves to portable storage. A sewing kit, for example, may be needed in the utility room or the bedroom. Baskets, boxes, trunks, and other small containers are all suitable choices.

ADVANTAGES
• Containers are often decorative.
• Available in all shapes and sizes.
• Boxes can be covered in coordinating fabrics.

DISADVANTAGES
• Need labeling for recognition of contents.
• Access difficult when stacked.
• Require somewhere to store containers.

STOCK CABINETS

Most commonly used in living areas and home offices, stock cabinets are a hybrid between built-in and freestanding furniture. They are available in many different designs, offering combinations of shelves, cubbyholes, and drawers.

ADVANTAGES
• Modules can be added as required.
• Can store many disparate items in one place.
• Possible to take with you if you move.

DISADVANTAGES
• A high-quality system is usually expensive.
• Standard sizes may not suit your room.
• Rarely look good in period homes.

SHELVING

THE MOST VERSATILE FORM of storage is shelving – whether freestanding, built-in, or within furniture, it is the most flexible way of accommodating objects. At its most basic, it is also the cheapest. Shelving that responds to the architecture of the room can be immensely appealing; if it is erected without any aesthetic consideration of the larger space, however, it can be detrimental. Select shelving according to the style of room, the nature of the objects to be stored, and whether or not you require flexibility.

POINTS TO CONSIDER

■ Analyze carefully what you intend to store on shelves. Measure your possessions by the yard, allowing for possible expansion.

■ Determine how large the objects to be stored are in relation to the shelf depth, and allow a few inches extra.

■ Do you want to build in lighting? Low-voltage can lights and spotlights are good for display; strip lights hidden behind a lipped front are also useful.

■ Assess how you will clean the shelves – this may affect your choice of material.

■ If shelving is to house electrical equipment, consider false backs to conceal the wiring or build power strips into the units.

WOOD

Hardwood is the most elegant, expensive material; softwood, such as pine, is less formal and cheaper. Timber must not clash with other wood in the room.

ADVANTAGES
• Has a natural beauty that wears well.
• Very sturdy and does not need edging.

DISADVANTAGES
• Some hardwoods may be difficult to obtain.
• While hardwood is strong, pine is less sturdy.

MDF (MEDIUM-DENSITY FIBERBOARD)

This is a versatile material, which when painted is often used as a substitute for wood. It is sturdy in short spans, and does not warp as much as solid wood.

ADVANTAGES
• Can be cut into different shapes easily.
• Available in many different thicknesses.

DISADVANTAGES
• Health risk, so wear a mask when cutting.
• Must be painted or varnished.

MELAMINE-FACED BOARD

Cheap and easy to wipe down, this is ideal for utility areas, kitchens, or bathrooms. If you want to upgrade it, it is possible to use a wood trim.

ADVANTAGES
• Impervious qualities good in wet situations.
• Inexpensive and practical.

DISADVANTAGES
• Needs careful application of edging detail.
• Can look cheap, particularly if shiny.

PLYWOOD

A cheaper alternative to wood, plywood is at present enjoying a fashionable image. It can be veneered in different woods, such as birch.

ADVANTAGES
• Can be extremely strong.
• Available in a waterproof variety.

DISADVANTAGES
• Feels like a substitute for more expensive wood.
• Edging must be carefully detailed.

TEMPERED GLASS

Glass shelves have a luminous quality, which can be enhanced by good lighting. They are particularly suitable for display purposes and in bathrooms.

ADVANTAGES
• Easy to wipe clean and does not stain.
• Decorative: can be clear, etched, or sandblasted.

DISADVANTAGES
• Expensive, as must be tempered.
• Shows fingerprints and may chip.

GALVANIZED METAL

Ideal for garages, greenhouses, and sheds, metal shelves are usually purchased in freestanding kit form, ranging from lightweight to heavy-duty shelving units.

ADVANTAGES
• Some kits designed for specific items, e.g., tools.
• Heavy-duty units can take a lot of weight.

DISADVANTAGES
• Will corrode over time and if damaged.
• Stylistically restrictive.

SHELF SUPPORTS

There are two basic types of built-in shelving: fixed shelves, which are often custom built; and adjustable shelves, which are usually available as a ready-made system and are more flexible, since the heights can be altered. Below are some of the supports available: choice must be guided by the shelf material, the load, and the style of room.

FIXED SUPPORTS

WOODEN BATTENS
A good, basic support for shelving in an alcove or recess; make sure that the battens stop short of the outer edges of the shelf to make them less obtrusive.

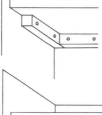

HIDDEN HARDWARE
D-shaped brackets attached to the walls slot into the short sides of the shelf and are hidden. An ideal minimalist solution for display shelving.

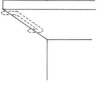

FIXED BRACKETS
These come in various forms, from a basic metal bracket to designer versions, as shown here. They do not need the support of side walls.

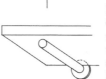

ADJUSTABLE SUPPORTS

SLOTS AND DOWELS
Suitable for short shelf spans between two walls; the shelf rests on dowels plugged into holes at the sides. Inobtrusive, so ideal with glass shelving.

STRIPS AND CLIPS
Same principle as above, but saves drilling the holes and gives more flexibility. Metal strips are attached to the side walls and shelves rest on metal clips.

RAILS AND BRACKETS
Good for large spans in utilitarian sites, brackets that slot into vertical tracks are very flexible, easy to install, and do not need side walls for support.

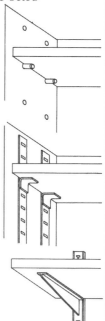

SHELF SPANS

The load a shelf can carry depends on the type of material used, its thickness, and the distance between supports. For short shelves, a support at either end is sufficient, but for longer spans you may need to add some intermediate ones. The chart below shows the maximum span to allow between supports for medium loads, such as light books or china. For heavier loads, you will need less distance between supports. If your drill goes in with little resistance, your wall might not be able to bear heavy loads.

MATERIAL	THICKNESS	DISTANCE BETWEEN SUPPORTS
Wood	⅝in (15mm) ⅞in (22mm) 1⅛in (28mm)	20in (50cm) 35in (90cm) 42in (106cm)
Glass Not suitable for heavy loads	¼in (6mm) ⅜in (10mm) ⅝in (15mm)	8in (20cm) 16in (40cm) 16in (40cm)
MDF **(Medium-density fiberboard)**	⅝in (15mm) ¾in (18mm) 1in (25mm)	20in (50cm) 28in (70cm) 35in (90cm)
Melamine-faced board	⅝in (15mm) ¾in (18mm)	16in (40cm) 24in (60cm)
Plywood	½in (12mm) ¾in (18mm) 1in (25mm)	16in (40cm) 24in (60cm) 32in (80cm)

DRAWERS AND PULL-OUTS

THE MAIN ADVANTAGE of drawers and pull-outs is that you can make the best use of the depth of a cabinet, avoiding dark or inaccessible corners where possessions could be overlooked. There is, however, a temptation to fit too much into drawers, a problem that can be addressed with a system of division and organization: as a general rule, do not fill them more than two-thirds full. A mixture of shallow and deeper drawers works well in most rooms. Bear in mind that drawers are more expensive than shelves.

WICKER BASKETS

Though rustic in origin, baskets that convert shelves into makeshift drawers suit both rural and urban situations. Suitable for vegetables, toys, and linens.

ADVANTAGES
• Can be lifted out onto countertop.
• Allow natural air circulation.

DISADVANTAGES
• Difficult to clean.
• Poor-quality baskets do not last long.

POINTS TO CONSIDER

■ Assess the objects you intend to store in terms of three-dimensional measurements; consider whether you might need to stack things within a drawer.

■ How do you want the drawers constructed – with runners or traditional drawer construction? Choose handles to suit the weight of the drawer or pull-out. If you

are having many small drawers, finger slots might be better than handles.

■ Consider the cost of traditional drawers versus wire baskets or other less expensive alternatives.

■ Select pull-outs according to the type and weight of the objects you want to store.

SMALL DRAWERS

Rows of small, square drawers are often designed into kitchens, but less expensive versions are also available for use in children's rooms and home offices.

ADVANTAGES
• Good for sorting small items.
• Small scale popular with children.

DISADVANTAGES
• Need some form of labeling.
• Expensive to build in.

SHALLOW DRAWERS

Drawers that are shallow impose order, as they encourage sorting and do not allow deep piles to build up. They are useful in the home office for stationery.

ADVANTAGES
• Items at bottom are not overlooked.
• Objects are easy to retrieve.

DISADVANTAGES
• More drawers are inevitably more expensive.
• Do not accommodate bulky items.

DEEP DRAWERS

A number of deep drawers are always useful, particularly in the bedroom for bulky items such as sweaters, and in the kitchen for baking pans and table linen.

ADVANTAGES
• Accommodate many different objects.
• Allow for stacking of items.

DISADVANTAGES
• Can quickly become disorganized.
• Items at bottom may be overlooked.

TIERED DRAWERS

Normally found only in more expensive kitchens, tiered drawers are very useful for cutlery (shallow drawers) and pots and pans (deeper drawers).

ADVANTAGES
• Make maximum use of drawer depth.
• Facilitate selection of objects.

DISADVANTAGES
• Expensive feature to install.
• Lower tray unsuitable for frequently used items.

DRAWER ORGANIZERS

Plastic boxes, a simple cutlery tray, or more sophisticated modular organizers can be inserted into any drawer to bring order to the contents.

ADVANTAGES
• Small objects are easy to locate.
• Disparate items kept in separate compartments.

DISADVANTAGES
• Standard widths may not fit your drawers.
• Compartments may not suit your requirements.

WIRE BASKETS

A cheaper alternative to drawers, wire baskets are contained in a floor-mounted stand or built into runners. They are available in many different sizes.

ADVANTAGES
• Good ventilation for food and clothes.
• Contents are visible when closed.

DISADVANTAGES
• May distort easily and come off runners.
• Can look cheap.

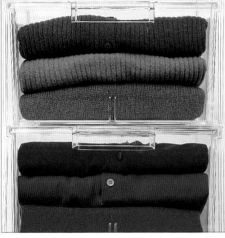

PLASTIC DRAWERS

Transparent and translucent drawers are useful throughout the house. They vary in cost: usually the more expensive the drawers, the sturdier they are.

ADVANTAGES
• Can see contents without opening drawers.
• Easy to keep clean.

DISADVANTAGES
• Poor-quality drawers do not survive heavy use.
• Surface scratches easily.

CORNER CAROUSELS

A built-in lazy susan allows you to make use of corner space that would otherwise be wasted. Some models pull out of the cabinet for even better access.

ADVANTAGES
• Maximize space in kitchen.
• Rotating shelves provide plenty of storage.

DISADVANTAGES
• Difficult to clean behind some models.
• Mechanism may not work smoothly.

PULL-OUT PANTRIES

Tall, narrow cabinets that pull out are very practical in a kitchen. The contents can be seen at once, and items do not "disappear" on deep shelves.

ADVANTAGES
• Highly efficient use of space.
• Items are easy to retrieve.

DISADVANTAGES
• More expensive than ordinary shelves.
• Wire baskets are difficult to clean.

CONCEALMENT

CONCEALING IS A MAJOR ELEMENT in storage. Some items, though practical and frequently used, may detract from the aesthetic harmony of a room. Others might not actually need concealing, just protection from dust. You may also want storage that keeps personal belongings out of sight. Generally speaking, the majority of objects need to be concealed but should still be accessible.

POINTS TO CONSIDER

■ Establish the reason for concealing items – for practicality, privacy, or aesthetics.

■ Try to anticipate how often you will want access to your concealed possessions. If you need them frequently, choose a method that requires minimum effort.

■ Take into account the amount of space required: side-hinged doors need a minimum of 24in (60cm) clearance in front of them.

■ Do you require part-time concealment? If you need constant access to the objects and want to cover them up only occasionally for cosmetic reasons, blinds, screens, tambour shutters, and curtains tend to offer the most useful methods of concealment.

■ Consider the practicalities, such as cleaning advantages and cost: avoid methods relying on a complicated mechanism unless you can afford the best quality.

FABRIC-FRONTED DOORS

To achieve a softer, more rustic look, replace solid door panels with wire mesh and pleated fabric. Particularly suitable for kitchens, bedrooms, and living areas.

ADVANTAGES
• Fabric design can tie in with other furnishings.
• Material can be changed as desired.

DISADVANTAGES
• More difficult to clean than solid doors.
• Side-hinged doors need clearance when open.

TAMBOUR SHUTTERS

Based on the pull-down principle of garage doors, tambour shutters hide items, such as kitchen appliances, that are often used but best concealed.

ADVANTAGES
• Useful for instant clean-up.
• Neat and do not intrude on the work surface.

DISADVANTAGES
• Only suitable for modern-style kitchens.
• Expensive and sometimes difficult to source.

RETRACTABLE DOORS

Doors that slide back along the depth of kitchen cabinets are completely hidden, leaving open space; when closed, they conceal the work area.

ADVANTAGES
• Allow dramatic transformations of view.
• Large areas of untidiness quickly hidden.

DISADVANTAGES
• An expensive, custom-made solution.
• Heavy doors need good-quality runners.

FOLD-BACK DOORS

This is a space-saving solution for tight corners, or in areas where you do not want the doors of a cabinet to protrude beyond a certain point in the room.

ADVANTAGES
• Do not need much clearance space.
• Fairly inexpensive solution.

DISADVANTAGES
• Central joints and hinging can be unattractive.
• Poor-quality models can come off tracks.

GLASS-FRONTED DOORS

Glass cabinets are particularly effective for storing glass and china. Sandblasted glass gives the same lucidity but offers a degree of opacity for less tidy owners.

ADVANTAGES
• Easy to clean.
• Display as well as protect contents.

DISADVANTAGES
• Items must be neatly arranged.
• Glass shows fingerprints.

TOP-HINGED DOORS

Most cabinets are side hinged, but in some cases top-hinged doors are more practical and look better, for example, when a cabinet is wider than it is tall.

ADVANTAGES
• Useful for cabinets above normal reach.
• Can make use of space above a doorway.

DISADVANTAGES
• Require a catch to hold in open position.
• Awkward to operate above a certain height.

SLIDING DOORS

Most commonly used in closets and cabinetry, sliding doors are particularly useful where there is restricted clearance space for open doors.

ADVANTAGES
• Save space as doors do not open into room.
• Discreet and unobtrusive.

DISADVANTAGES
• Only half of contents are visible when open.
• Dirt collects on tracks.

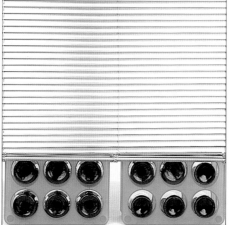

CURTAINS

The most basic method of concealing is to curtain off an area that can be used for storage, such as under a table, or an alcove or section of the room.

ADVANTAGES
• Inexpensive and easy to achieve.
• Give a soft, informal look.

DISADVANTAGES
• Inconvenient to keep pulling back curtains.
• Not appropriate in formal rooms.

VENETIAN BLINDS

Particularly suited to minimalist or high-tech interiors, Venetian blinds offer a quick and inexpensive way of cordoning off large areas of storage.

ADVANTAGES
• Flexible slats give good visibility.
• Available in metal and wood in many colors.

DISADVANTAGES
• Cleaning of blinds is labor-intensive.
• May be difficult to operate.

FOLDING SCREENS

Screens offer temporary concealment of objects. They are available in many materials, and give a new dynamic to the architecture of the room.

ADVANTAGES
• Totally flexible and movable.
• Can contribute to decorating plans.

DISADVANTAGES
• No protection from dust and grime.
• Some materials may be difficult to clean.

PLANNING YOUR STORAGE

STORAGE MUST BE PLANNED to suit you. Try to resist buying a piece of furniture without careful consideration, since it may not accommodate your needs. First, establish what you want to store, then work on a design solution. Even if it involves only one wall, you will need to measure and draw up a plan to scale.

MEASURING

Before embarking on a plan, assess exactly how much you need to store. This involves literally measuring your possessions by the foot, remembering to allow for future additions. You must also measure the room: accurate measurements of the floor area and walls will help you decide exactly where to locate storage, and enable you to work out whether it will fit comfortably into the available space. You will need a tape measure, notepad, pencil, and stepladder.

❶ SKETCH THE ROOM
Stand in the center of room and, with a soft pencil, draw a rough sketch of the floor area in a notepad. Draw in the outlines of any existing fixed furniture and features, such as doors and windows, that need to be considered in your design.

❷ PLOT THE DIMENSIONS
Measure the length and width of the room, then measure each of the wall lengths in turn. Do not assume that the walls are symmetrical. At this stage, ignore surface detail such as baseboards. Jot down the dimensions in your notepad.

❸ MEASURE THE HEIGHT
Stand facing one wall, and draw a rough sketch. Include any features such as doors, windows, or alcoves. Details, such as moldings, are not important yet. Standing on a stepladder, measure the wall height from floor to ceiling. Note it down on the sketch.

❹ PLOT SET FEATURES
Record the height and width of doors, baseboards, and ceiling moldings, plus other architectural features such as door moldings and windowsills. Make a note of any places that you do not want to obstruct. Repeat steps 3 and 4 for each wall.

DRAWING SCALE PLANS

Once you have measured and completed rough sketches of the room, draw your sketch to scale (*see p15*), using the graph paper provided at the back of the book, a ruler, a T-square, and drawing pens. Concentrate on the room plan first, to decide the best area for storage, then draw elevations for each wall where storage will be located – you may find that there are several options.

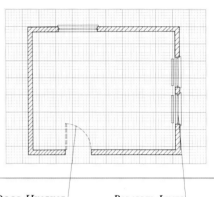

DOOR HINGING
A curved line indicates the directional swing of the door.

PARALLEL LINES
These show the window as a source of light.

❶ DRAWING A ROOM PLAN
Referring to the rough sketch for measurements, accurately plot the four perimeter walls to scale on graph paper. Next, plot features that are pertinent to planning, such as door swings and position of windows. Remember to show fireplaces, radiators, and other permanent features.

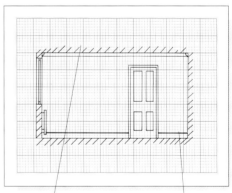

MOLDING
The line parallel to the ceiling indicates the height of the molding.

BASEBOARD
The line parallel to the floor indicates the height of the baseboard.

❷ DRAWING AN ELEVATION
Using your measurements of heights, draw an elevation of each relevant wall to scale on graph paper. Add details of fixed architectural features, such as baseboards, moldings, and door and window frames, as well as any existing electrical outlets in the room.

DESIGNING YOUR STORAGE

After you have read the Introduction (*pp6–15*) and relevant room chapters, and have drawn your measured survey to scale, you will be equipped to design storage to suit your needs. Explore how various arrangements work by laying a piece of tracing paper over the scaled-up room plan or elevations with masking tape, and drawing on the storage elements. Keep the architectural features of the room in mind, and explore different alternatives. Do not be afraid to experiment – most good solutions tend to be refinements of earlier, less developed attempts. Once you have decided which design is most successful, draw it directly onto the graph paper, using a T-square and ruler.

DESIGN TIPS

■ Always bear in mind the architectural characteristics and proportions of your room, and make sure that your design enhances rather than interferes with them.

■ Avoid building too close to major features such as doors and windows.

■ Try to achieve a regular plan for your room, once the storage has been added: unless you have complete confidence in your design skills, symmetry of composition usually works best.

■ Bringing the ceiling molding and baseboards in front of built-in units gives a more integrated, architectural feel, as if the storage has been sculpted out of the walls.

ROOM PLANS

REJECTED PLAN ▽
This design disperses the shelving in two different areas, which is divisive and choppy. The storage cuts into the room, destroying its proportions and making it too narrow at one end.

FLOOR AREA
The space between the blocks of shelving is not sufficient for both seating and access to shelves.

SUCCESSFUL PLAN ▽
This plan respects the proportions of the room, leaving space clear around the windows for seating or dining. It has a sense of order, with the door centered on one window and the bookcase across from the other windows.

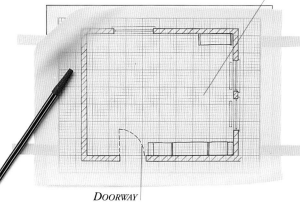

DOORWAY
The side of the bookcase butts up against the doorway, making entrance awkward.

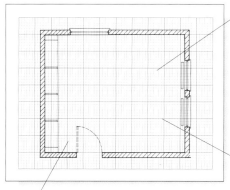

NATURAL LIGHT
The windows are unobstructed by storage, allowing full exploitation of light areas.

SEATING AREA
A large area is left clear for seating, close to the natural light of the windows.

CLEARANCE
The bookcases are sited on the side wall, with a generous margin in front of the door.

ELEVATIONS

REJECTED ELEVATION ▽
The wrong wall has been chosen for this elevation, since the result looks lopsided and crowded. The bookshelves are too close to the door, and they jut out awkwardly into the room.

MOLDING
The molding, following the line of the shelves, makes an awkward, irregular shape.

SUCCESSFUL ELEVATION ▽
This wall is a considerably better choice: it provides a very efficient run of bookshelves, which does not interfere with the surrounding architectural features. The unit looks integral to the room, not like something that has been added on as an afterthought.

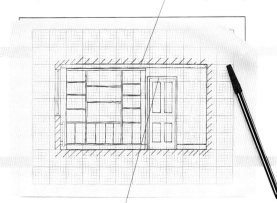

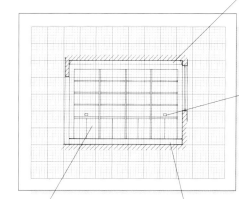

MOLDING
The molding, which has been brought in front of the unit, integrates the storage into the architecture.

ELECTRICAL OUTLETS
The outlets are raised to counter height for lighting and electrical equipment.

DOORWAY
The height of the door does not align with any of the shelves in the bookcase.

CABINETRY
Storage offers cabinets for concealment as well as shelves for display.

BASEBOARD
The baseboard runs in front of the unit, framing it architecturally.

USEFUL ADDRESSES

The following directory of useful names and addresses will help you source the storage items needed for every room in your home.

PROFESSIONAL ASSOCIATIONS

AMERICAN LIGHTING ASSOCIATION
P. O. Box 420288
World Trade Center, Suite 10046
Dallas, TX 45342-0288
Tel: (214) 698-9898
Tel: (800) 605-4448
Fax: (214) 698-9899
National association of lighting manufacturers.

AMERICAN SOCIETY OF INTERIOR DESIGNERS
608 Massachusetts Ave. NE
Washington, DC 20002-6006
Tel: (202) 546-3480
Fax: (202) 546-3240
National association of interior designers.

NATIONAL KITCHEN AND BATH ASSOCIATION
687 Willow Grove Street
Hackettstown, NJ 07840
Tel: (800) 401-NKBA
Tel: (800) 843-6522
National association of kitchen and bathroom designers, and manufacturers of kitchen and bathroom products.

GENERAL FURNITURE

ADVANCED FURNITURE OUTFITTERS
P. O. Box 741
Bryan, OH 43506
Tel: (800) 501-1110
Fax: (800) 501-2220
http://www.afo.com
Furniture for home offices, entertainment centers, kitchens, bedrooms, and more; mail and phone orders.

BALLARD DESIGNS
1670 DeFoor Avenue NW
Atlanta, GA 30318-7528
Tel: (800) 367-2775
Accessories for the home; call for catalog.

THE BARTLEY COLLECTION LTD.
65 Engerman Avenue
Denton, MD 21629
Tel: (800) 787-2800
Reproduction furniture kits; call for catalog.

BED, BATH, AND BEYOND
620 Avenue of the Americas
New York, NY 10011
Tel: (212) 255-3550
Storage items for bedrooms, bathrooms, and the rest of the house; call for catalog and nearest store location.

BLOOMINGDALE'S
P. O. Box 8096
Mason, OH 45040
Tel: (800) 555-7467
Furniture and storage items for the home; call for catalog and nearest store location.

THE BOMBAY COMPANY
P. O. Box 161009
Fort Worth, TX 76161-1009
Tel: (800) 829-7789
Fax: (817) 347-8291
Furniture and accessories for the home; call for catalog and retail stores.

CRATE & BARREL
Tel: (888) 249-4158
Home furnishings and equipment; phone and mail orders; call for catalog and retail stores.

DECORATORS DIMENSIONS
217 Martling Ave.
Tarrytown, NY 10591
Tel: (914) 631-9326
Fax: (914) 631-4815
Furniture, including ready-to-assemble items; phone and mail orders.

DOOR STORE
116 East 38th St.
New York, NY 10016
Tel: (800) 433-4071
Bookshelves, platform beds, and other products for the home; call for retail locations.

EDDIE BAUER
P. O. Box 97000
Redmond, WA 98073-9700
Tel: (800) 789-1386
Fax: (206) 869-4629
Furniture and accessories for the home; call for catalog and retail stores.

ETHAN ALLEN
Ethan Allen Drive
Danbury, CT 06811
Tel: (800) 273-2191
Furniture and storage items for the home; call for nearest store location.

GOLDEN OLDIES
P. O. Box 541625
Flushing, NY 11354
Tel: (800) 435-0547
Specialists in antique armoires, many refurbished to hold televisions, stereos, and other electronics.

GOODWILL INDUSTRIES
A useful source for used furniture of every type. Consult Yellow Pages for store locations.

HOLD EVERYTHING
see listing under General Storage Systems

HOME DEPOT
Corporate Offices
2727 Paces Ferry Road
Atlanta, GA 30339
Tel: (800) 553-3199
Nationwide chain of home supply stores; call for catalog, information, and retail stores.

HOME FURNITURE
65 Cedar Pointe Dr.
Unit 800
Barrie, Ontario, Canada L4N 5R7
Tel: (705) 721-7333
Fax: (705) 721-5026
Bedroom furniture and more; mail and phone orders.

IKEA
185 Discovery Dr.
Colmar, PA 18915
Furniture and storage products for every room. Write for catalog and store locations.

LAND'S END
1 Land's End Lane
Dodgeville, WI 53595
Tel: (800) 356-4444
Furniture and accents for the home; call for catalog.

LEVENGER
420 Commerce Dr.
Delray Beach,
FL 33445-4696
Tel: (800) 544-0880
Fax: (800) 544-6901
Bookshelves and other items
for the home library; call
for catalog.

LEVITZ FURNITURE
6111 Broken Sound
Parkway NW
Boca Raton, FL 33487
Tel: (888) 800-2000
http://www.levitz.com
National chain of furniture stores;
call for nearest location.

L.L. BEAN, INC.
Freeport, ME 04033
Tel: (800) 221-4221
Furniture accent pieces; call for catalog.

MACY'S
P. O. Box 8079
Mason, OH 45040
Tel: (800) 456-2297
Furniture and storage items for the home; call
for catalog and nearest store location.

POMPANOOSUC MILLS
P. O. Box 238
E. Thetford, VT 05043
Tel: (800) 841-6671
Television and media cabinets, bookcases, and
other hardwood furniture; call for catalog.

POTTERY BARN
Mail Order Department
P. O. Box 7044
San Francisco, CA 94120-7044
Tel: (800) 922-5507
Fax: (415) 421-5153
Accessories for the home; call for catalog and
retail stores.

SALVATION ARMY
(Western 13 states)
Tel: (800) 378-7272
A nationwide source for used furniture and
household items. Check Yellow Pages or call
for nearest retail location.

SPIEGEL
P. O. Box 182556
Columbus, OH 43218-2557
Tel: (800) 527-1577
Fax: (800) 442-6697
http://www.spiegel.com
Furniture and accessories for the home;
call for catalog.

THIS END UP
4609 Carolina Avenue
Building H
Richmond, VA 23222
Tel: (800) 627-5161
Furniture for every room;
call for retail locations.

**WICKER
WAREHOUSE, INC.**
195 South River Street
Hackensack, NJ 07601
Tel: (800) 989-4253
Tel: (201) 342-6709
Fax: (201) 342-1495
Wicker furniture; phone and mail orders.

WORKBENCH
180 Pulaski Street
Bayonne, NJ 07002
Tel: (800) 656-7891
Bookshelves, storage units, and other
furniture; call for catalog and retail stores.

KITCHEN

COLONIAL GARDEN KITCHENS
Dept CGZ4183
Hanover, PA 17333-0066
Tel: (800) 323-6000
Kitchen equipment, appliances, and gadgetry;
phone and mail orders.

FIELDSTONE KITCHENS
P. O. Box 109
Northwood, IA 50459
Tel: (800) 339-5369
Cabinetry for the kitchen and other rooms;
call for literature and retail stores.

PIER 1 IMPORTS
Tel: (800) 447-4371
Small items for the kitchen; call for retail
store locations.

PINE FACTORY
P. O. Drawer 672
Ashland, VA 23005
Tel: (804) 796-9156
Pine kitchen furniture; phone
and mail orders.

POTTERY BARN
Mail Order Department
P. O. Box 7044
San Francisco, CA 94120-7044
Tel: (800) 922-5507
Kitchen furniture and accessories; phone and
mail orders; call for catalog and retail stores.

RENOVATOR'S SUPPLY
P. O. Box 2515
Conway, NH 03818-2515
Tel: (800) 659-2211
Specialists in reproduction fittings, lighting,
etc for kitchens and bathrooms.

YIELD HOUSE
P. O. Box 2525
Conway, NH 03818-2515
Tel: (800) 659-0206
Largest furniture mail-order house in US.
Kits available for home builders.
Call for catalog.

BATHROOM

AMERICAN STANDARD, INC.
P. O. Box 6820
One Centennial Plaza
Piscataway, NJ 08855
Tel: (800) 752-6292
Tel: (908) 980-3000
Bathroom fixtures, bath accessories.

AQUAWARE AMERICA, INC.
One Selleck Street
Norwalk, CT 06855
Tel: (800) 527-4498
Tel: (203) 853-3678
Fax: (203) 855-1360
Bathroom fixtures, accessories.

**BURGESS INTERNATIONAL BATH
FIXTURES**
Burgess International
27120 Trolley Drive
Taylor, MI 48180
Tel: (313) 292-7070
Fax: (313) 292-9793
Bathroom fixtures, accessories.

CHAMBERS
P. O. Box 7841
San Francisco, CA
94120-7841
Tel: (800) 334-9790
Fax: (415) 421-5153
Storage supplies for
bathroom and bedroom;
call for catalog.

KOHLER CO.
444 Highland Drive
Kohler, WI 53044
Tel: (800) 456-4537
Tel: (414) 457-4441
Bathroom fixtures in many styles and colours; call or fax for catalog, product information, and referrals to retail sources.

WHITEHAUS COLLECTION
589 Orange Ave.
West Haven, CT 06516
Tel: (800) 527-6690
Fax: (800) 694-4837
Coordinated bath suites, specialty plumbing products.

CHILD'S ROOM

BELLINI
8201 Quaker Ave.
Kingsgate Center
Lubbock, TX 79424
Tel: (800) 785-1385
Children's furniture, including toy shelves, cribs that convert to day beds, and changing tables that change into bookshelves with hutches; call for retail stores.

JC PENNEY – FOR BABY
Catalog Division
Milwaukee, WI 53262-0370
Tel: (800) 322-1189
Fax: (800) 711-9624
Nursery furniture; call for catalog.

LITTLE TIKES CO.
P. O. Box 2277
Hudson, OH 44236-0877
Tel: (800) 321-0183
Children's bookshelves, toy boxes, and headboards with storage space; call for catalog.

STEP 2 CO.
P. O. Box 2412
Streets Boro, OH 44241
Tel: (800) 347-8372
Children's bookshelves, toy boxes, and other products with storage space; call for catalog and retail stores.

HOME OFFICE

DOORS AND DRAWERS
64722 CR 27
Goshen, IN 46526
Tel: (219) 533-3509
Fax: (219) 533-3509
Stock storage systems for the home and home office.

METAMORPHOSIS
1347 Spring St.
Atlanta, GA 30309
Tel: (800) 700-9141
Fax: (404) 378-8141
Ergonomic computer furniture; mail and phone orders.

CABINETRY

ADELPHI CUSTOM CABINETRY
P. O. Box 10
Robesonia, PA 19551
Tel: (800) 922-3101
Custom cabinetry for bedrooms, living rooms, family rooms, kitchens, etc.

ARISTOKRAFT, INC.
PO Box 420
Jasper, IN 47547
Tel: (812) 482-2527
Cabinetry for kitchens and other rooms; call for retail outlets.

KRAFTMAID CABINETRY INC.
16052 Industrial Parkway
Box 1055
Middlefield, OH 44062
Tel: (800) 766-4523
http://www.kraftmaid.com
Cabinetry for kitchens and other rooms; call for literature and retail stores.

MERILLAT INDUSTRIES, INC.
MASCO Corp.
P. O. Box 1946
5353 West US 223
Adrian, MI 49921
Tel: (517) 263-0771
Fax: (517) 263-4792
Custom cabinetry for kitchens, living rooms/family rooms, etc.

SNAIDERO INTERNATIONAL USA, INC.
201 West 132nd Street
Los Angeles, CA 90061
Tel: (310) 516-8499
Fax: (310) 516-9918
http://www.snaidero.it
Custom cabinetry for the home.

STARMARK CABINETRY
P. O. Box 84810
Sioux Falls, SD 57118
Tel: (800) 594-9444
Cabinetry for kitchens and other rooms; call for literature and retail outlets.

GENERAL STORAGE SYSTEMS

ACE HARDWARE CORPORATION
2200 Kensington Court
Oak Brook, IL 60521
Tel: (800) 223-8663
Closet hardware and related storage items; call for retail locations.

ALSTO'S HANDY HELPERS
P. O. Box 1267
Galesburg, IL 61402
Tel: (800) 447-0048
Fax: (800) 522-5786
Storage products and small items for the home; call for catalog.

THE ANTIQUE HARDWARE STORE
1C Mathews Court
Hilton Head Island, SC 29926
Tel: (800) 422-9982
Medicine cabinets, umbrella stands, and other storage-related items; call for catalog.

CALIFORNIA CLOSET COMPANY
Tel: (800) 873-4264
Stock storage systems; custom designs available; call for product information and referrals to retail outlets.

CLOSETTEC
55 Providence Highway
Norwood, MA 02062
Tel: (617) 769-9997
Fax: (617) 769-9996
Storage design; components for closet storage systems.

HOLD EVERYTHING
Tel: (800) 421-2264
(catalog requests)
Tel: (800) 421-2285
(customer service)
Closet storage, multiple storage systems for the home; call for catalog, product information, and referrals to your nearest retail store.

KNAPE AND VOGT MFG. CO.
2700 Oak Industrial Drive NE
Grand Rapids, MI 49505
Tel: (800) 253-1561
Tel: (616) 459-3311
Fax: (616) 459-3290
Designers and manufacturers of closet storage systems.

OUTWATER PLASTICS INDUSTRIES, INC.
4 Passaic Street
Wood Ridge, NJ 07075
Tel: (201) 340-1040
Tel: (800) 631-8375
Fax: (800) 888-3315
outwater<\@>outwater.com
http://outwater.com
Designers and manufacturers of closet storage systems.

RACK MAGIC
R. C. Purnell Co.
4 Maynard Circle
Old Saybrook, CT 06475
Tel: (806) 388-2681
Fax: (800) 388-5068
Closet storage systems; home organizing products; shelving and storage, etc.

REV-A-SHELF, INC.
2409 Plantside Drive
Jeffersontown, KY 40299
Tel: (800) 626-1126
Tel: (502) 499-5835
Fax: (502) 491-2215
http://www.revashelf.com
Shelving systems and storage products.

RUBBERMAID PRODUCTS
1147 Akron Road
Wooster, OH 44691
Tel: (330) 264-6464
Storage products for every room; call for retail stores.

SCHULTE CORP.
12115 Ellington Court
Cincinnati, OH 45239
Tel: (800) 669-3269
Tel: (513) 489-9300
Fax: (513) 247-3389
Closet and home storage systems.

SPACE MAKERS CLOSET INTERIORS
600 Wylie Road
Marietta, GA 30067
Tel: (770) 952-3455
Fax: (770) 422-6054
Closet design; home storage systems.

SPACEMETRICS INC.
885 Market Street
Oregon, WI 53575
Tel: (608) 835-8850
Fax: (608) 835-8860
Closet and home storage systems.

LIGHTING

ELKAY MANUFACTURING COMPANY
2222 Camden Court
Oak Brook, IL 60521
Tel: (630) 574-8484
Specialized and general lighting products.

GOLDEN VALLEY LIGHTING
274 Eastchester Drive
High Point, NC 27262
Tel: (800) 735-3377
Specialized and general lighting products.

TASK LIGHTING CORPORATION
P. O. Box 1090
910 East 25th Street
Kearney, NE 68848-1090
Tel: (800) 445-6404
Tel: (308) 236-6707
Fax: (308) 234-9401
Designers and manufacturers of lighting systems.

SPECIALTY PRODUCTS

FORMICA CORPORATION
10155 Reading Road
Cincinnati, OH 45241-5729
Tel: (800) 367-6422
Tel: (513) 786-3533
Fax: (513) 786-3024
Laminate surfacing and other products for cabinets, etc.

HIDE-AWAY IRONING BOARDS
5563 S. 104th East Ave.
Tulsa, OK 74146
Tel: (800) 759-4766
Tel: (918) 493-6566
Fax: (918) 494-6866
Ironing boards that store in/against walls, in closets, etc.

J & M AIR, INC.
189 South Bridge Street
Somerville, NJ 08876
Tel: (908) 707-4040
Fax: (908) 707-0447
Custom stainless steel installations.

MARVEL INDUSTRIES
P. O. Box 997
233 Industrial Parkway
Richmond, IN 47375
Tel: (800) 428-6644
Tel: (317) 962-2521
Fax: (317) 962-2493
Undercounter half-keg beer dispensers.

SIMPLEX ACCESS CONTROLS
Division of Ilco Unican Corp.
2491 Indiana Ave.
Winson-Salem, NC 27105
Tel: (910) 725-1331
Fax: (800) 346-9640
Childproof cabinet locks; mechanical push-button locks.

WILSONART INTERNATIONAL
2400 Wilson Place
Temple, TX 76504
Tel: (800) 433-3222
Tel: (817) 778-2711
Fax: (817) 770-2384
Laminate surfacing and other products for countertops, c... ts. etc.

INDEX

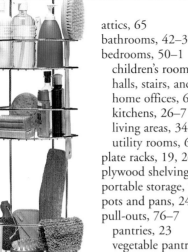

ACKNOWLEDGMENTS

AUTHORS' ACKNOWLEDGMENTS
Dinah Hall would like to thank:
Polly Boyd at Dorling Kindersley, for
patient editorial guidance. The urge to
clean out my kitchen cupboards as a
form of work displacement was even
stronger than usual when writing this
book. That it ever got written and my
cupboards remained chaotic can only be
due to Polly's firm hand.

Barbara Weiss would like to thank:
Everyone at the office for their great
patience during this project, in particular
Alastair Howe, Lisa Shell, and Kim
Katzen; Katherine Lennard, Vera Barrett,
Rebecca Silver, Zoë Crook, and Rita
Wolff, for very kindly allowing us to
photograph their houses; Marianne
Majerus, for the loan of photographs;
Kilkelco Construction, for all their help
and hard work.

PUBLISHER'S ACKNOWLEDGMENTS
Dorling Kindersley would like to thank:
Sarah Gaventa, for her help with
locations; Charlotte Davies and Clive
Hayball, for their support and advice;
Angeles Gavira and Simon Maughan, for
editorial assistance; Martin Hendry and
Ina Stradins, for design assistance; Hilary
Bird, for compiling the index; Robert
Campbell, for his technical support; Bob
Brown, for his set-building skills; Fran
and Mark Bussell and Simon Palmer, for
their fine accommodation and props; and
Al Deane and Karen Thomas, assistants
to Matthew Ward.

Thank you also to the following
owners who generously let us
photograph their homes: Vera
Barrett; Anthony and Julia
Collett; Katherine and Stephen
Lennard; Bella Pringle and
Richard Blair-Oliphant;
Rebecca and Simon Silver;
Barbara Weiss.

We are also grateful to those
who kindly supplied props:
Aero; Aria; Body Shop;
Bulldog Tools; C.P. Hart &
Sons Ltd; Christopher Wray;
Clifton Nurseries; The
CubeStore; Czech and Speake
Ltd; David Mellor; Decorative
Living; The Domestic Paraphernalia
Co; Dyson; Early Learning Centre;
Flymo; Freemans Catalogue; Galt Toys
Ltd; General Trading Company; Geo F.
Trumper; Graham and Green; Habitat;
Herbert Johnson; The Holding Company;
Homebase Ltd; Ikea Ltd; Intersport; Key
Industrial Equipment Ltd; Lakeland
Plastics Ltd; Metropolis; Mothercare;
Neal Street Remedies; Newcastle
Furniture Company Ltd; Old Painted
Pine Furniture; On Yer Bike; Panasonic;
Paperchase; Paula Pryke Flowers; Peter
Farlow; The Pier; Purves & Purves;
Reject Shop; Robert Dyas; Rosenthal
Studio-haus; Selfridges; Shaker; Sharps
Bedrooms; Siematic; Tie Rack; Toys 'R'
Us; Traditional Garden Supply Co; Tumi;
Wedgwood; Windrush Mill; Zanussi Ltd
(Fridge with Cool Check 21).

We would also like to thank those
companies who lent
us photographs: Aero
(Lizard CD rack 32);
American Appliance
Centre (drinks fridge
23); Bisley (shallow
drawers 76);
Bulthaup (bread-bin
drawer 21, under-
hob racks 24, small
drawers 76); Charles
Page (walk-in closet
8, 46, wardrobe with
sliding doors 79);
C.P. Hart & Sons
Ltd (basin with hand
towel rail 12, 39);
Crabtree Kitchens (food processor
storage unit 25); Habitat (clothes
tent 13, 47, mobile television unit
and CD storage 32, bathroom 36,

freestanding bathroom
shelving 39, modular unit
73); The Holding
Company (fabric shoe
pockets 49); Interlübke
(unit with fold-back doors
78); Keith de la Plain Ltd
(work station 59);
Newcastle Furniture
Company Ltd (utensils rack
25); Samuel Heath & Sons
(bath rack 38); Sub-zero
(refrigerated drawers 21).

ARTWORK
David Ashby 9, 25, 38, 47,
54, 75; John Egan 3, 26–7, 34–5, 42–3,
50–1, 56–7, 62–3, 65, 67, 69; Barbara
Weiss 70–1, 80–1.

PHOTOGRAPHY
All photographs by Peter Anderson and
Matthew Ward except: Tim Beddow /
The Interior Archive 8cm, 29br;
Dominic Blackmore / Ideal Home /
Robert Harding Syndication 59tr;
Bonhams London / Bridgeman Art
Library 6tl, 72tr; Andy Crawford 4bl,
5tr, 53tl, 53tr, 53br, 70–1c, 72cl, 74–5,
77tr, 77bl, 79cb, 79br; Christopher
Drake / Country Homes and Interiors /
Robert Harding Syndication 61br;
Michael Freeman 4tr, 6b, 37c, 73tl;
Rodney Hyett / Elizabeth Whiting and
Associates 65tl, 69tl; Cecilia Innes / The
Interior Archive 46tr; Ray Main 61tm;
Marianne Majerus 9br (designer Mary
Rose Young), 30l, 31br, 41tr, 41br
(designer Barbara Weiss), 55, 60bl, 66br
(designer Léon Krier); Jonathan
Pilkington / The Interior Archive 19tr,
22tr, 29bc, 65r; Paul Ryan / International
Interiors 10b (designer Lisa Corti), 20c
and 79bl (designer Frances Halliday),
60b (designer E. Dylan); Wayne Vincent
/ The Interior Archive 52 (designer
Lesley Saddington); Fritz von der
Schulenburg / The Interior Archive 7,
28, 44, 45bl, 54cl, 72bl; Andreas von
Einsiedel / Elizabeth Whiting and
Associates 66tr (architect Christian
Stocker); Jakob Wästberg / The Interior
Archive 58; Elizabeth Whiting and
Associates 23tl; Henry Wilson / The
Interior Archive 10t, 29c; Peter
Woloszynski / The Interior Archive 59bl;
ZuhauseWohnen / Camera Press 64.

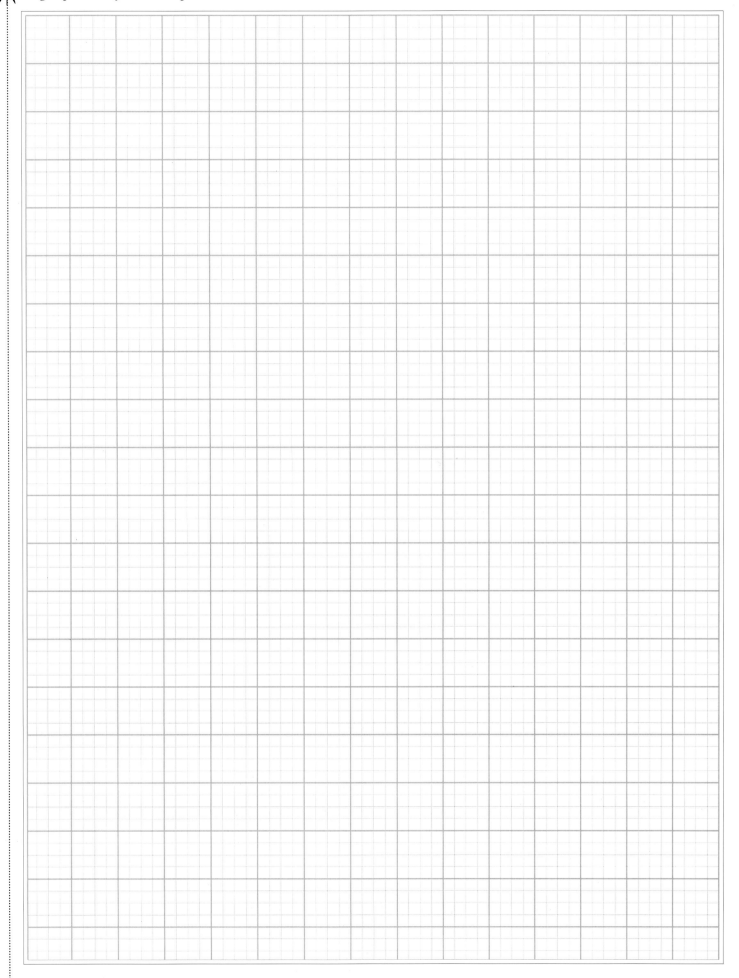

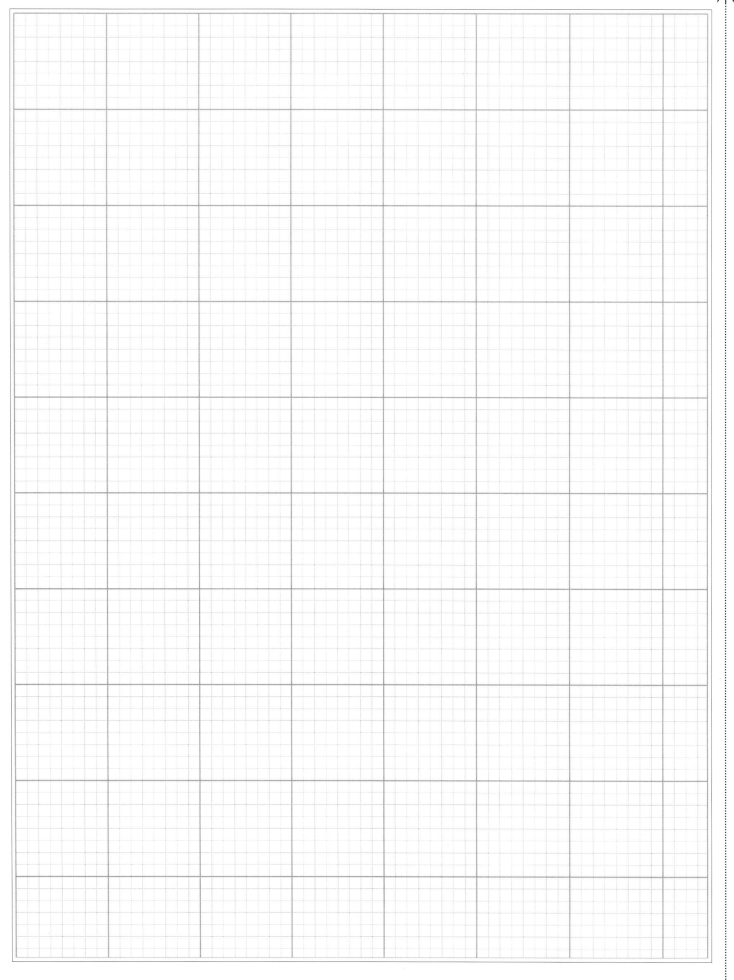

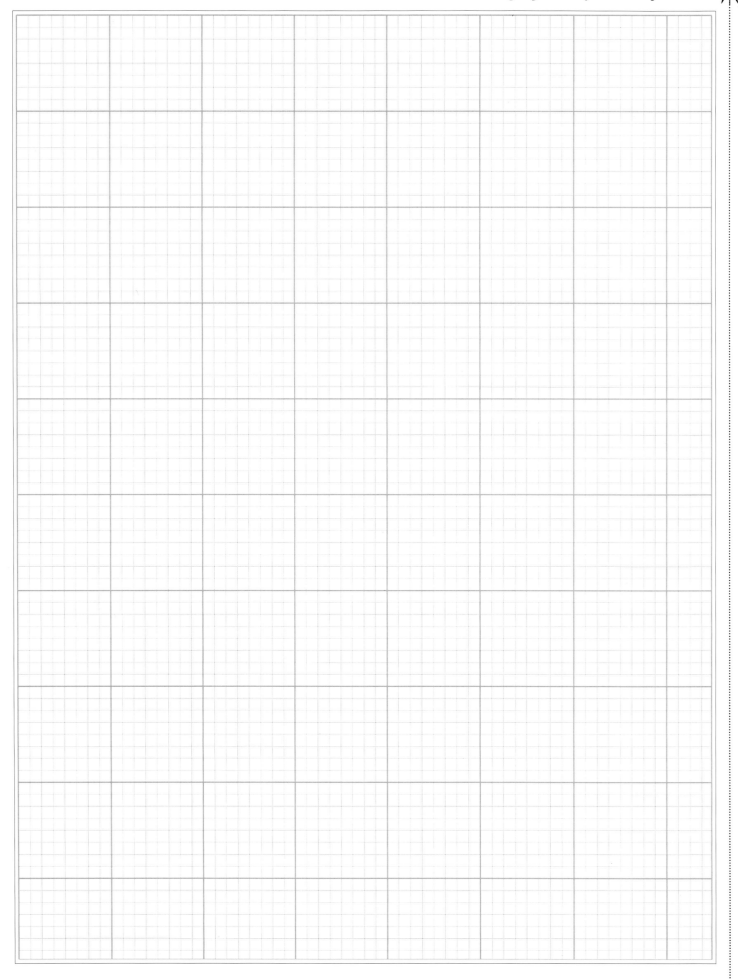

Large Squares = 1m • Small Squares = 10cm

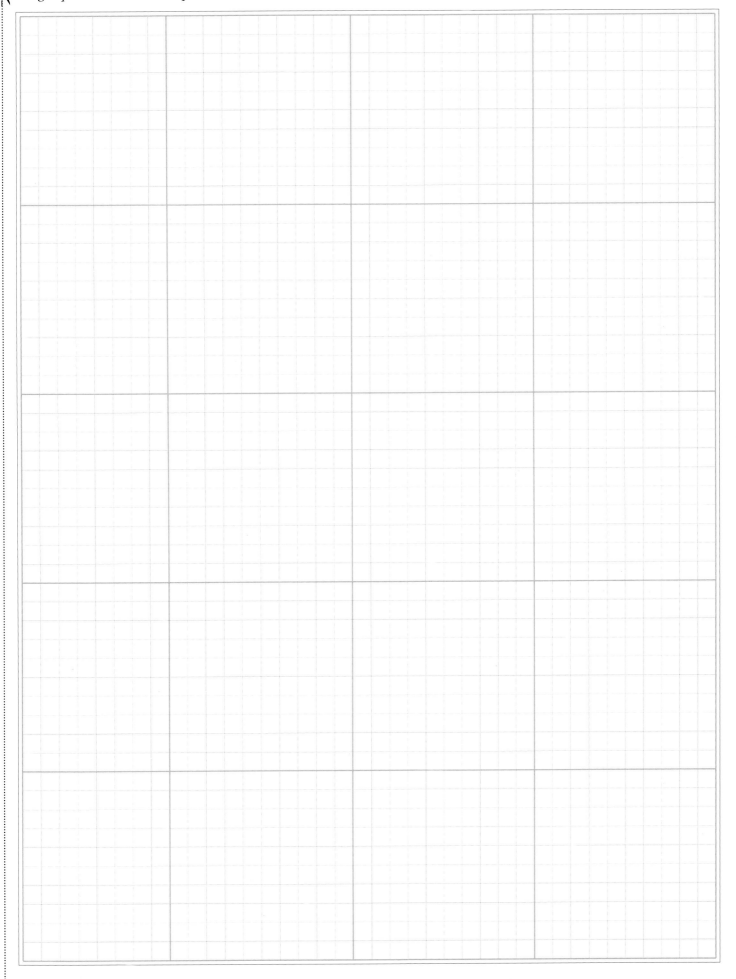